Edinburgh

COLLINS
Glasgow & London

First published 1990
Copyright © William Collins Sons & Company Limited
Published by William Collins Sons & Company Limited
Printed in Hong Kong
ISBN 0 00 435788-4

HOW TO USE THIS BOOK

Your Collins Traveller Guide will help you find your way around your chosen destination quickly and easily. It is colour-coded for easy reference:

The blue-coded 'topic' section answers the question 'I would like to see or do something; where do I go and what do I see when I get there?' A simple, clear layout provides an alphabetical list of activities and events, offers you a selection of each, tells you how to get there, what it will cost, when it is open and what to expect. Each topic in the list has its own simplified map, showing the position of each item and the nearest landmark or transport access, for instant orientation. Whether your interest is Architecture or Sport you can find all the information you need quickly and simply. Where major resorts within an area require in-depth treatment, they follow the main topics section in alphabetical order.

The red-coded section is a lively and informative gazetteer. In one alphabetical list you can find essential facts about the main places and cultural items - 'What is La Bastille?', 'Who was Michelangelo?' - as well as practical and invaluable travel information. It covers everything you need to know to help you enjoy yourself and get the most out of your time away, from Accommodation through Babysitters, Car Hire, Food, Health, Money, Newspapers, Taxis and Telephones to Zoos.

Cross-references: Type in small capitals - CHURCHES - tells you that more information on an item is available within the topic on churches. A-Z in bold - A-Z - tells you that more information is available on an item within the gazetteer. Simply look under the appropriate heading. A name in bold - Holy Cathedral - also tells you that more information on an item is available in the gazetteer under that particular heading.

Packed full of information and easy to use - you'll always know where you are with your Collins Traveller Guide!

Photographs by **Keith Allardyce** *and* **Bob Wood**

INTRODUCTION

Cecil B de Mille could not have designed a better set for one of his epics. Edinburgh Castle, sitting proudly on its rock, dominates the city as it looks down on the elegance of the New Town and the rugged timelessness of the Old Town. However, for all this grandeur, Edinburgh is a charming place which retains a small town feel.

The sense of history is almost palpable. Wander down the winding streets and cobbled closes of the Old Town and you may almost expect to meet a medieval housewife going about her business only a stone's throw away from modern-day living and glaring souvenir shops. Yet Edinburgh's very beginnings are difficult to trace.

By the 5thC Pictish tribes had occupied the castle rock and realised its defensive potential. Other conquerors followed but the city's destiny was assured when Malcolm Canmore moved his court there from Dunfermline in the 11thC. Thereafter Edinburgh flourished.

At the heart of the city is the castle which houses a military museum and the Scottish Regalia. On a clear day the view from the esplanade over the city and the outlying area is spectacular. At one o'clock every day local people can be spotted checking their watches as a gun is fired from the artillery platform. Each year the esplanade is also used for the Military Tattoo, an extravaganza featuring bands and display teams from all over the world. The sight and sound of the massed pipes and drums on a chilly September night will never be forgotten.

By the 16thC most of the Old Town had been built and the street names of today point to their earlier use. The Lawnmarket was where cloth was sold; the Grassmarket was the place for agricultural products and Candlemaker's Row is self-explanatory!

In contrast to these streets is the elegant New Town. In the 18th C the city's officials decided the time had come for expansions and a competition was held to find a designer. The winner was an unknown 23-year old architect, James Craig. His plan was classic and grand and the results can be seen today in the beautiful streets which are his legacy. To gain a better idea of life for the wealthy inhabitants of Edinburgh at the time, visit the Georgian House in Charlotte Square which has been lovingly restored by the National Trust for Scotland. There is furniture in the style of Sheraton and Chippendale, porcelain by Wedgewood and there are paintings by Ramsay.

Although the sense of history is ever present Edinburgh has not stood still. After the Second World War a major arts event was mooted and out of that was born the annual International Festival, first held in 1947. At the end of August and in early September it attracts leading companies from all over the world. There are plays, reviews, mimes, recitals and operas. As if that were not enough there are also Fringe events. And with a Jazz Festival and a Film Festival as well the choice is staggering.

In other fields too Edinburgh has excelled. It takes a leading role in the banking and financial world, its university is renowned - especially for the teaching of science and medicine - and the major law courts of Scotland are in the city. Although Dr Johnson once wrote that the best sight for a Scotsman was the road to England, the converse is now true. Increasingly, people from the South are making their way north, attracted by living in a place where the quality of life is hard to match in other British cities.

For the tourist, however, the problem remains not what to see and do but how to choose what to leave for another visit. Away from the galleries, the museums, and the Palace of Holyroodhouse, there are the shops. Rightly, Princes Street is well-known. Its setting is unrivalled but unfortunately the majority of its shops are now chain stores, with one exception being Jenners, which offers a wide range of traditional and high-quality goods. In many of the side streets there are small individual shops and if you are interested in taking home some history the antique shops in St Stephen Street should prove interesting.

If you tire of the city itself, there are many villages nearby worth visiting. Probably one of the most picturesque is Cramond. The Cramond Inn is a popular stopping-off point and Cramond House is said to have been the setting for Robert Louis Stevenson's House of Shaws in *Kidnapped*. However, the village nestling around the River Almond estuary is worthwhile just for a stroll.

There are also many pubs and restaurants to relax in during the evening after a day's sightseeing. Leith is fast becoming the Covent Garden of Edinburgh and Rose Street, behind Princes Street, has long been renowned for the number of pubs along it. Many have tried to have a drink in each one of a night, few have succeeded.

For history, atmosphere and sheer enjoyment there are few places which will reward the visitor as well as this proud capital.

Joanna MacDonald

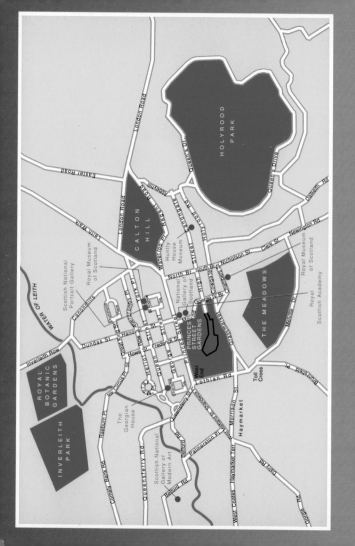

NATIONAL GALLERY OF SCOTLAND The Mound.
• 1000-1700 Mon.-Sat., 1400-1700 Sun. •Free.
One of the best of Europe's smaller galleries. Fine collection of Impressionists.

ROYAL SCOTTISH ACADEMY The Mound.
• 1000-1900 Mon.-Sat., 1400-1700 Sun. •Admission £1.20, 50p child.
Built in 1826 to Playfair's Greek Temple design. Exhibitions of well-known foreign artists during Festival.

ROYAL MUSEUM OF SCOTLAND Chambers St.
• 1000-1700 Mon.-Sat.,1400-1700 Sun. •Free. Buses 2, 3, 5, 7, 8, 21, 23, 27, 31, 33, 37, 41, 42, 46.
Decorative arts, archaeology, ethnography, natural history, geology, technology, science. Lovely glass-roofed main hall.

ROYAL MUSEUM OF SCOTLAND 1 Queen St.
• 1000-1700 Mon.-Sat., 1400-1700 Sun. •Free.
Traces the history of Scotland from Stone Age to modern times.

SCOTTISH NATIONAL PORTRAIT GALLERY 1 Queen St.
• 1000-1700 Mon.-Sat.,1400-1700. Sun. •Free.
Portraits of famous past Scots and history of Scottish photography.

SCOTTISH NATIONAL GALLERY OF MODERN ART
Belford Road. •1000-1700 Mon.-Sat., 1400-1700 Sun. •Free. Buses Eastern Scottish C13.
20thC art, including Hockney, Hepworth, Picasso and Moore.

HUNTLY HOUSE MUSEUM 142 Canongate, Royal Mile.
• 1000-1800 Mon.-Sat. Closed Sun. •Free. Buses 1, 6.
Local history, pottery, shopsigns, trade artefacts and other relics.

THE GEORGIAN HOUSE 7 Charlotte Square.
• 1000-1700 Mon.-Sat., 1400-1700 Sun. Closed Dec.-Mar. •£1.50
Georgian town house of c. 1800, lovingly restored in every detail.

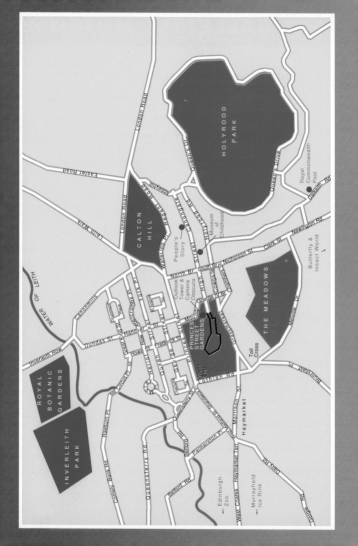

MUSEUM OF CHILDHOOD 42 High St., Royal Mile.
•1000-1800 Mon.-Sat. Closed Sun. •Free. Buses 1, 6, 34, 35.
Toys, dolls, games, and all the paraphernalia of childhood through the ages.

EDINBURGH ZOO Corstorphine Road.
•0900-1800 Mon.-Sat., 0930-1800 Sun. •£2.50 adult, £1.25 child.
Buses 2, 12, 26, 31, 85, 86.
Famous for its colony of penguins. Penguin Parade every day in summer.

PEOPLE'S STORY Canongate Tolbooth, 163 Canongate.
•1000-1800 Mon.-Sat. •Free. Buses 1, 6, 34, 35.
Exhibition showing the daily life of local citizens through the ages.

OUTLOOK TOWER & CAMERA OBSCURA Royal Mile.
•0930-1600 Mon.-Fri., 1000-1800 Sat.-Sun. •£1.70, 80p child. Buses
1, 6, 23, 27, 30, 34, 35, 40, 41, 42, 46.
Optical system projects live image of city.

BUTTERFLY & INSECT WORLD Dobie's Garden Ctre, Lasswade.
•1000-1730 daily. Closed Nov.-Mar. •£1.75 adult, £1.00 child, Buses
Lrt 3, Eastern Scottish 80, 81 from St Andrew Sq.
Glasshouse with tropical plants, butterflies, stick insects, scorpions, etc.

COMMONWEALTH POOL 21 Dalkeith Road.
•1430-2000 Mon.-Thu., 1200-2000 Fri., 1000-1500 Sat.-Sun.
•£1.00 for 5 rides. Buses 2, 12, 21, 33, 82, 83.
Exciting, enclosed waterslides, built onto swimming-pool complex.

MURRAYFIELD ICE RINK Riversdale Crescent.
•Daily 1430-1630. •80p-£1.10. Skate hire 40p. Buses 2, 12, 26.
Ice-skating is popular in Scotland. Tuition available.

FIRTH OF FORTH

Portobello

Leith

Old Town

New Town

Newhaven

Stockbridge

Dean Village

Water of Leith

Union Canal

Cramond

OLD TOWN *Tall, tenement buildings, many dating from the 15th-17thC, and narrow closes characterize Edinburgh's atmospheric Old Town. See* **Old Town**, **WALK 1**.

NEW TOWN *Built 1767-1840 to relieve overcrowding in the Old Town.Broad streets and sweeping terraces, spacious gardens and elegant Georgian architecture combine to create the classical beauty of the New Town. See* **New Town**, **WALK 2**.

DEAN VILLAGE (Bus 41 to Dean Bridge, then walk down Bell's Brae) *A picturesque village, dating from the 12thC, that grew up around the mills on the Water of Leith. See* **WALK 4**.

LEITH (Buses 2,9,10,12,16,22,25,34,35,87,89) *For centuries Leith has been the Scottish capital's sea-port. Now it is a fashionable area with new restaurants and wine bars springing up along the waterfront.*

STOCKBRIDGE (Buses 24,28,29,34,35,41A) *No more than a rural hamlet until the 18thC when it was enveloped by the growing city, Stockbridge retains a village atmosphere with its busy shops and tea-rooms, huddled around the bridge over the Water of Leith.*

PORTOBELLO (Buses 2,12,15,26,42,46,85,86,89) *Dating from the mid-18thC, Portobello was Victorian Edinburgh's seaside resort, with bracing sea air and miles of golden sands. The promenade, beach and amusements still draw plenty of summer visitors today.*

NEWHAVEN (Buses 9,10,11,16,22) *Rows of cottages cluster behind Newhaven Harbour in this former fishing village. It supplied the city with oysters and herring in the 18th and 19thC. There is a local museum in Victoria School, Main St.*

CRAMOND (Buses 18,41) *Picture-postcard village at mouth of River Almond on west edge of city. It was once a busy industrial area based on milling grain and making iron, paper and cloth. A popular spot for weekend picnickers and strollers.*

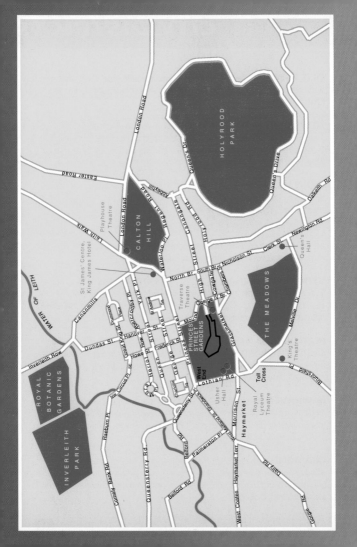

ROYAL LYCEUM THEATRE Grindlay St.
•Box office Mon.-Sat. 1000-1800. •Tickets £2.50-£7.00.
Buses 2, 12, 9, 10, 11, 15, 16, 18, 34, 35.
The city's principal venue for drama. 1200 seat auditorium, built in 1883.

PLAYHOUSE THEATRE 18-22 Greenside Place.
•Box office Mon.-Sat. 1000-1800. •Tickets £6-£13.
Buses 4,9,10, 11,15,16,22,25,34,35,42,46,43,44.
Scottish Opera, Scottish Ballet, and big-name rock concerts. There is a 3500 seat auditorium.

KING'S THEATRE 2 Leven St.
•Box office Mon.-Sat. 1000-1800. •Tickets £2-£11.
Buses 9,10,11,16,23,27,45,47.
Opera, ballet, drama, musicals, variety shows, Christmas pantomimes.

USHER HALL Lothian Road.
•Box office Mon.-Sat. 0900-1700. •Tickets £2.70-£11.50.
Buses 9,10,11,15,16,18,34,35,62.
Lovely Victorian building, recently renovated, classical concerts with the Scottish Chamber Orchestra and Scottish National Orchestra.

QUEEN'S HALL 89 Clerk St.
•Box office 1000-1700. •Tickets £2.20-£9.60.
Buses 2,3,5,7,12,24,31,33,40,41,42,46,51.
Regular classical, jazz, folk and pop concerts.

TRAVERSE THEATRE 112 West Bow, Grassmarket.
•Box office Tues.-Sat. 1000-2000, Sun. 1800-2200. •Tickets £4.50.
Buses 2,12,23,24,27,40,41,42,45,46.
Small but famous theatre staging new works by contemporary Scottish and international writers.

KING JAMES HOTEL St James' Centre. •Shows Sun.-Fri. 1845-2200. Closed Sat & Nov.-Apr. •£23.00 a head, tickets incl. dinner.
Scottish dinner and cabaret, with haggis supper and toast to Burns.

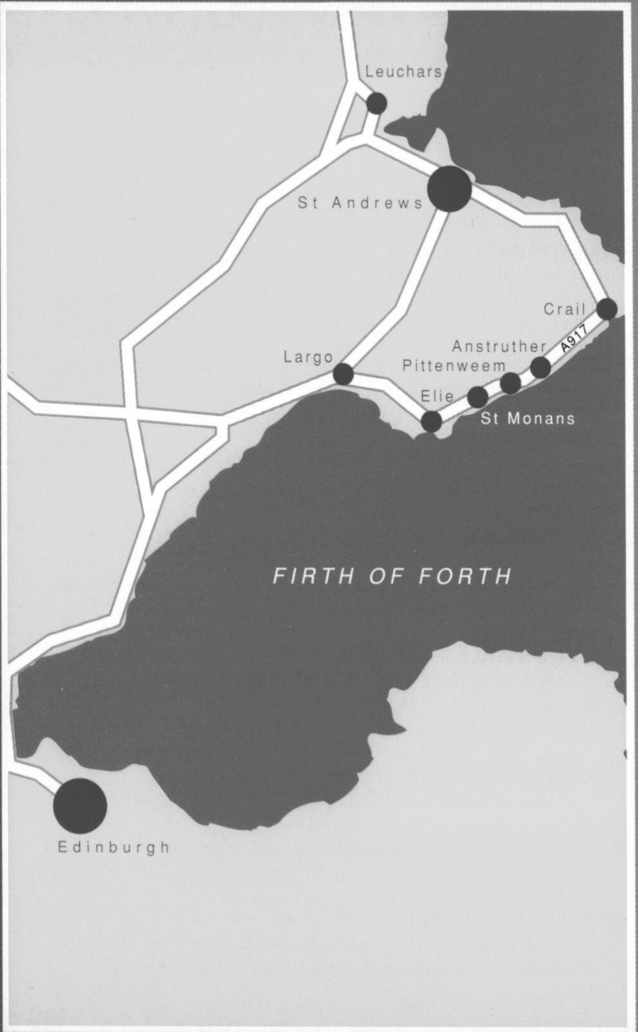

Leuchars

St Andrews

Crail

Anstruther
Pittenweem

Largo
A917

Elie
St Monans

FIRTH OF FORTH

Edinburgh

St Andrews

Time required: 1day.

St Andrews is about 72 km from Edinburgh, accessible by car, or regular bus service. The nearest railway station is at Leuchars, about 6 km away (trains from Waverley Station).

The ancient city of St Andrews is a pretty seaside town, rich in historical associations. Founded by King David I in 1140, it became Scotland's ecclesiastical capital with the building of St Andrews Cathedral. Begun in 1161, the Cathedral flourished for four centuries until it was ransacked by the Reformers in 1599 after which it fell into ruin. The ruins are open to the public, and the 12thC St Rule's Tower offers excellent views over the town. Nearby are the ruins of 13thC St Andrews Castle with its sinister bottle-dungeon hewn out of the solid rock. The Cathedral, Castle and neighbouring Museum are open 0930-1900 Mon.-Sat., 1400-1900 Sun. (closed at 1600 Oct.-Nov.). Museum also closes 1230-1330.

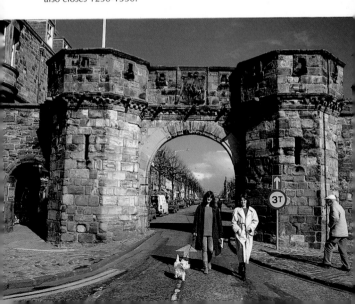

St Andrews also possesses Scotland's oldest university, dating from 1411, and lays claim to being the home of golf. The world-famous Old Course lies on the Links to the north and is open to visitors.

Other attractions include the Botanical Gardens, the fine sandy beaches, and many pleasant coastal walks. Tourist Information Centre, 78 South St, St Andrews, tel: (0334) 72021.

From St Andrews, return to Edinburgh by the A917 and visit the picturesque fishing villages of the East Neuk of Fife. Crail has charming stone-built houses with distinctive pantile roofs and crow-stepped gables, the 12thC church of St Mary's, a museum, and an attractive harbour. Further on is Anstruther with the Scottish Fisheries Museum, the North Carr Lightship Museum, and a restored 19thC fishing boat. There are boat-trips to the Isle of May to see the seals and sea-birds. The next village is Pittenweem, with its Flemish architecture, and a daily market selling freshly caught fish. St Monans has a 14thC fishermen's church, the ruins of Newark Castle, and a ruined windmill. Elie is an ideal spot for sailing, windsurfing and swimming and Largo is the birthplace of Alexander Selkirk, the real-life castaway whose story provided the basis for Robinson Crusoe.

Tourist Information Offices at Harbourhead, Anstruther, tel: (0333) 310628; The Museum, 11 Marketgate, Crail, tel: (0333) 50869.

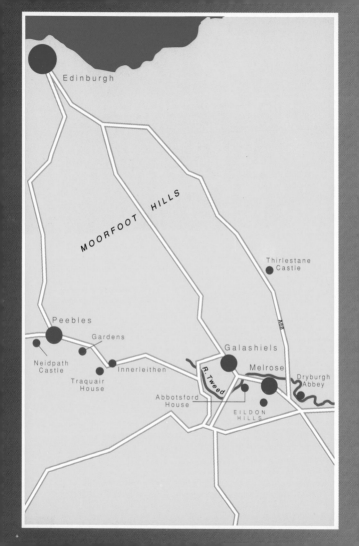

Scott Country

Time required: 1 day.

The scenic Borders countryside to the south of Edinburgh is historically associated with the life and work of Sir Walter Scott. Private transport required.

The Royal Burgh of Peebles (37 km from Edinburgh) is a picturesque little town situated on the River Tweed, with a local museum, and the ruins of the 13thC Cross Kirk. There are beautiful walks along the river, especially to the west towards Neidpath Castle. Open Easter & 30 Apr. -9 Oct., 1000-1300, 1400-1700 Mon.-Sat., 1300-1700 Sun. Admission 75p, 20p child.

Near Innerleithen is Traquair House, dating from the 12thC, which claims to be the oldest inhabited house in Scotland. You can admire its historic furniture, embroideries and books, and explore the cellars and secret stairways, or relax with a glass of Traquair Ale, brewed by the 20th Earl of Traquair in his 18thC private brewhouse. There are also craft workshops and a tea-room and restaurant. Traquair House is open Easter & 1 May -30 Sep., 1330-1730 daily (1030-1730 from 1 July -14 Sept.).

The next mill town is Galashiels, and nearby is Abbotsford, the house which Sir Walter Scott built and lived in from 1812 until his death in 1832. See his study, his library with its rare books, the drawing-room with hand-painted Chinese wallpapers, and his dining-room overlooking the Tweed. Open 21 Mar. -31 Oct., 1000-1700 Mon.-Sat. , 1400-1700 Sun. Admission £1.30, 65p child.

Beyond Melrose is the beautiful Dryburgh Abbey, founded in 1140. Sir Walter Scott is buried within the walls. A mile from here, on the B6356 road, is the famous 'Scott's View', a beauty spot overlooking the Tweed valley.

Follow the A68 back towards Edinburgh, stopping to visit Thirlestane Castle, an ancient Border stronghold guarding the invasion route to the capital. See the impressive stateroom with its ornate plaster ceiling and wood panelling, and the Border Country Life Exhibition, which displays aspects of life in the Borders from the earliest times onward. Open Thur. & Sun. Easter, May, Jun. & Sept., only; daily except Sat. July & Aug.: grounds open 1200-1800, Castle & Exhibition open 1400-1700. Admission £2, £1.50 child.

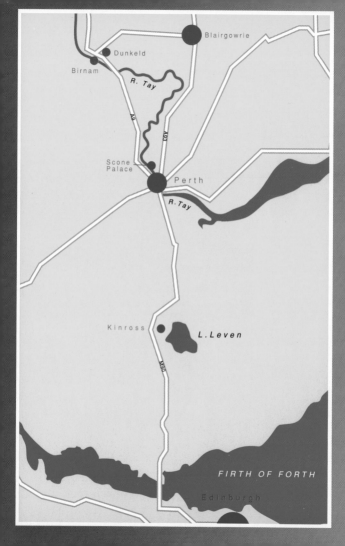

Perth

Time required: 1 day.

The 'Fair City' of Perth lies on the River Tay, 67 km north of Edinburgh, accessible by car via the Forth Road Bridge and M90 motorway, or by regular bus and train services.

En route from Edinburgh is Loch Leven, famed for the quality of its trout-fishing, the gatherings of wildfowl, and the historic Loch Leven Castle. The Castle is an island fortress, accessible by boat from nearby Kinross. Mary, Queen of Scots, was held captive here in 1567.

The city of Perth is known variously as the Fair City, the Heart of Scotland, and the Nation's Crossroads. In olden times this was the lowest bridging point on the River Tay. You can visit St Ninian's Cathedral, dating from 1849, with its magnificent stained-glass windows and beautiful rood-screen, and the much older St John's Kirk, founded in 1126. On the western edge of the city is the splendid, 15thC Huntingtower Castle, whose fine architecture includes a remarkable painted ceiling. Open, 0930-1900 Mon.-Sat. Apr. -Sep., 1400-1900 Sun.; Oct-Mar. closes at 1600. Admission 50p, 25p child. Other attractions in town include Balhousie Castle with its Black Watch Regimental Museum, the Fair Maid's House, Branklyn Garden, and the Perth Museum & Art Gallery. And don't miss the chance of a walk on Kinnoul Hill, with lovely views over the Tay valley. Tourist Information Office, The Round House, Marshall Place, tel: (0738) 38353.

Two miles out of town on the A93 road to Blairgowrie is the famous Scone Palace, where for 700 years the Kings of Scotland were crowned. The collections on view inside the Palace include French furniture, china, ivories and Vernis Martin. There is an excellent restaurant and gift-shop, and the extensive gardens and woods include a world-famous Pinetum with the original Douglas Fir. Open 0930-1700 Mon.-Sat., 1330 Sun. (1000 in July & Aug.) and 1700 Easter-mid Oct. Admission to house and grounds £2.50, £2.00 child; grounds only £1.25, £1.00 child. Family ticket £9.00.

21 km north of Perth on the A9 are the attractive villages of Dunkeld and Birnam. Dunkeld was the ecclesiastical capital of Scotland in the 9thC, and has its Cathedral and many finely preserved old houses in a picturesque riverside setting. There are also many pleasant walks to be enjoyed in the surrounding woods.

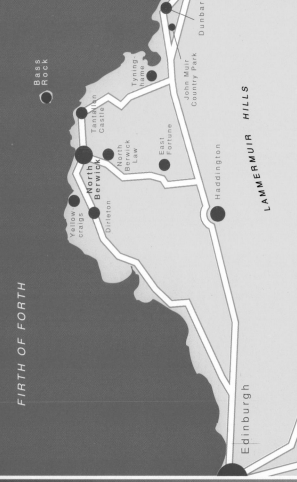

East Lothian

Time required: 1 or 2 days.
The coastline and countryside stretching east from Edinburgh has many attractions for the visitor, including beaches, golf courses, nature trails and historic houses and castles. North Berwick and Dunbar are accessible by bus and train, and Haddington by bus only.

The Royal Burgh of Haddington is an attractive market town with over 100 Listed Buildings of historic or architectural interest, including the 14thC Collegiate Church of St Mary, the Town House, built by William Adam in 1748, with its distinctive spire, and Mitchell's Close, a 17thC tenement building restored in 1967, with many of its original features preserved.

North Berwick is a traditional seaside resort with lots of character, overlooked by the prominent conical hill of Berwick Law (187 m/613 ft), which is visible from parts of Edinburgh on a clear day. There is a footpath to the summit, which bears a Napoleonic watch-tower and a whalebone arch. Boat trips run from North Berwick's harbour to the Bass Rock with its lighthouse and huge gannet colony (14,000 pairs of birds).Tourist Information: Quality St, tel: (0620) 2197.

A few miles to the west of North Berwick is the pleasant village of Dirleton, with its impressive 13thC castle, and access to the golden strand of Yellowcraigs beach, while to the south is the Museum of Flight at East Fortune. To the east of the town is the dramatic ruin of Tantallon Castle, with walls over 4m thick, perched on a precarious cliff-top site. Castle is open 0930-1900 Mon.-Sat., 1400-1900 Sun.; closes at 1600 Oct.-Mar.

Further east along the coast is the pretty, twin-harboured fishing town of Dunbar, with the crumbling ruins of a 15thC castle dominating the harbour entrance. The town is the birthplace of John Muir (1838-1914), little known in Scotland but famed throughout America as the father of the nature conservation movement and founder of National Parks. His childhood home in the High Street is now a museum, and the John Muir Country Park to the west of the town provides cliff-top walks and nature trails. Nearby, Tyninghame House Gardens are open to the public in the summer months, offering colourful herbaceous borders and peaceful wooded and terraced gardens. Tourist Information: The Town House, High St., Dunbar, tel: (0368) 63353.

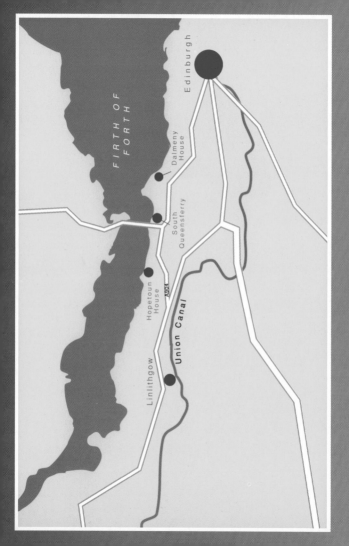

Linlithgow

Time required: half to 1 day.

The town of Linlithgow is 27 km west of Edinburgh, and easily accessible by car, bus or train. Private transport is recommended for visiting Hopetoun and Dalmeny Houses.

Linlithgow grew up around the 15th to 17thC Palace which still dominates the town, although today the structure is nothing more than a shell. It occupies a lovely setting on the shore of Linlithgow Loch. Mary, Queen of Scots, was born here in 1542. Nearby is the restored 15thC church of St Michael's, with its controversial aluminium crown spire, added in 1964. The Union Canal passes through the town, and originally linked Edinburgh with the Forth & Clyde Canal at Falkirk. The canal was closed in the 1930s, but is now being restored for the use of pleasure craft. Boat trips are available from Easter until September. There is a Canal Museum at the Basin, housed in the old stable that onced served the horses used to tow barges along the canal. Museum open Easter-Sept., 1400-1700 Sat. & Sun. only. Admission free. There are pleasant walks along the towpath, especially to the west where you will find the spectacular Avon Aqueduct (built 1819-22), which carries the canal 26 m/86 ft above the gorge of the River Avon. North of the A904 road from Linlithgow to South Queensferry lies the magnificent mansion of Hopetoun House, home of the Marquis of Linlithgow, and the finest Scottish example of the work of architect William Adam. Admire the sumptuous interiors, with priceless collections of paintings, china, tapestries, costumes and decorations, and stroll in the beautiful gardens overlooking the Firth of Forth. Open daily 1000-1730, Easter and May-Sep.

On the far side of South Queensferry from Hopetoun is another stately home, Dalmeny House, seat of the Earls of Rosebery. The present house dates from 1815, and was built in the Tudor-Gothic style. The impressive art collection within includes 18thC French furniture, Goya tapestries and paintings by Gainsborough, Reynolds, Raeburn and Millais. The 5th Earl was an authority on the life of Napoleon, and in addition to writing a book about the French Emperor, collected many objects, paintings and pieces of furniture connected with him. In spring, the gardens surrounding the house provide a colourful display of rhododendron and azalea. Open May-Sep, 1400-1730 Sun.-Thur.

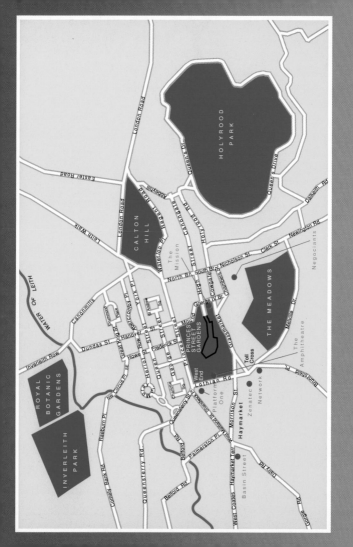

PLATFORM ONE Rutland St.
• Check listings for times and bands. • Admission usually free.
Comfortable bar, offers sessions of jazz, folk and R&B.

BASIN STREET Haymarket Terr.
• Check listings for times and bands. • Admission usually free. Buses
2,3,4,12,21,22,25,26,28,29, 31,33,43,44.
Pleasant pub with regular live jazz from local bands.

NEGOCIANTS Bristo Sq., Teviot Row.
• Check listings. • Free. Buses 2,23,24,27.
A busy wine bar with live music downstairs on most nights.

THE AMPHITHEATRE 31 Lothian Rd.
• 2200-0400 Fri., 2330-0400 Sat., 2200-0300 Sun. • £2.00-£4.00, half-
price before 2300. Buses 9,10,11,15,16,18,34,35,62.
The city's top nightclub. Over-21s only, no denim. Good laser show.

NETWORK 3 West Tollcross.
• 2200-0330 Thu., 2230-0400 Fri.-Sat., 2230-0330 Sun. • £2.00-£3.00.
Buses 9,10,11, 15,16,18,23,24,27,30,62,72,79.
Recently refurbished, newly opened, with bright lights and great music.

THE MISSION Victoria St.
• 2230-0300 Wed.-Sun. • £2.00. Buses 2,12,23,24,27,40,41,42,45,46.
Two separate discos playing soul, hiphop and funk.

ZENATEC 56 Fountainbridge.
• 2200-0400 Fri.-Sat., 2200-0330 Sun. • £3.50-£4.00. Free before 2230
on Fri. Buses 2,12,30,34,35.
Comfortable, relaxed, up-market club. Smart dress, and over-21s only.

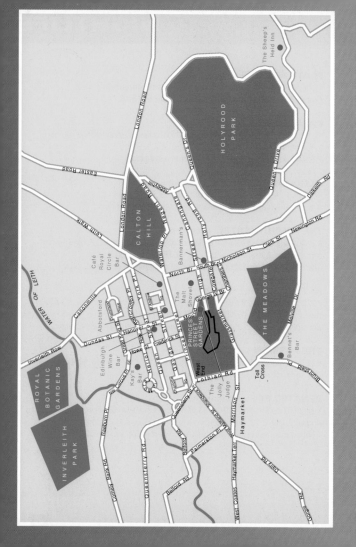

BENNET'S BAR 8 Leven St.
Buses 9,10,11,16,23,27,45,47. Food at lunchtime.
Beautiful Victorian interior with stained-glass windows, ornamented ceiling.

ABBOTSFORD Rose St.
Traditional pub. Richly carved 'island' bar, leather benches.

BANNERMAN'S 55 Niddry St., Cowgate.
Buses 3,5,7,21,30,31,33,87.
Flagstone floors and barrel-vault ceiling. Youngish crowd, many students.

THE MALT SHOVEL 13 Cockburn St.
Comfortable, intimate lounge with a wide choice of beers, malt whiskies.

EDINBURGH WINE BAR 110 Hanover St.
 Buses 8,9,23,27.
Friendly and relaxed New Town watering hole.

THE SHEEP'S HEID Causeway, Duddingston Village.
Buses 4,42,43,44,45,46,47.
*Delightful old-fashioned inn at the foot of Arthur's Seat. There is a skittles
alley at the back.*

THE JOLLY JUDGE 7a James Court, Lawnmarket, Royal Mile.
Buses 23,24,27,30, 34,35,40,41,42,45,46,89.
A small, snug, low-ceilinged hostelry down an Old Town close.

KAY'S BAR 39 Jamaica St.
Buses 24,28,29,41A.
*Former New Town wine-merchant's shop converted into a cosy lounge,
with classical music in the background. Off the beaten track, but worth
seeking out.*

CAFE ROYAL CIRCLE BAR West Register St.
*Large, stylish Victorian pub, with long oval bar in middle, and attractive tile
portraits of engineers and inventors on wall.*

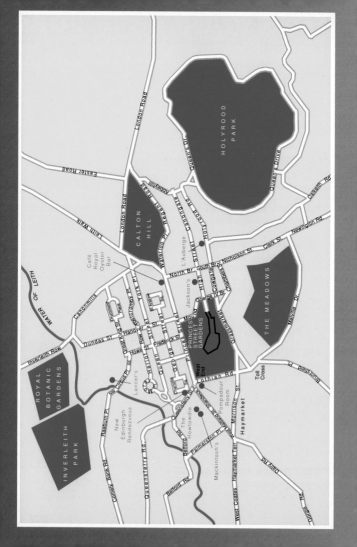

POMPADOUR ROOM Caledonian Hotel, Princes St.
•1200-1400, 1930-2230 Mon.-Fri., 1930-2230 Sat.-Sun. •Expensive.
Traditional Scottish fare at lunch, international cuisine in the evenings.

THE HOWTOWDIE 27a Stafford St.
•1200-1400, 1900-2300 Mon.-Fri., 1900-2300 Sat. Closed Sun.
•Expensive. Buses 2,12,26,29,31, 33,85,86.
Traditional Scottish cooking served in one of the city's best restaurants.

MACKINTOSH'S 24a Stafford St.
•Daily 1200-1400, 1800-2200. Buses 2,12,26,29,31,33,85,86.
•Expensive
An intimate restaurant with Art Nouveau decor, serving game and seafood.

JACKSON'S 2 Jackson's Close, 209 High St., Royal Mile.
•1200-1500, 1800-2230 Mon.-Sat. Closed Sun. •Moderate.
Buses 3,21,30,31,33,34,35,80,81,82.
Elegant restaurant, the menu shows Scottish and French influences.

L'AUBERGE 56-58 St Mary's St.
•1215-1400, 1845-2130. Closed Sun. Buses 1,6. •Expensive.
Genuine nouvelle cuisine can be enjoyed in this stylish French restaurant.

CAFE ROYAL OYSTER BAR 17a West Register St.
•1200-1400, 1900-2230. •Expensive.
The oldest seafood restaurant in Scotland. Interesting Victorian interior.

NEW EDINBURGH RENDEZVOUS 10a Queensferry St.
•1200-1400, 1730-2330 Mon.-Sat., 1300-2330 Sun. •Moderate.
Buses 18,19,29,34,35, 40,41,80,81,85.
Sample some of the best Pekinese cuisine in Scotland.

LANCER'S 5 Hamilton Place, Stockbridge.
•1230-1430, 1730-2300. •Moderate. Buses 24,29,34.
A wide selection of excellent Bengali and northern Indian cuisine and a variety of less expensive vegetarian dishes.

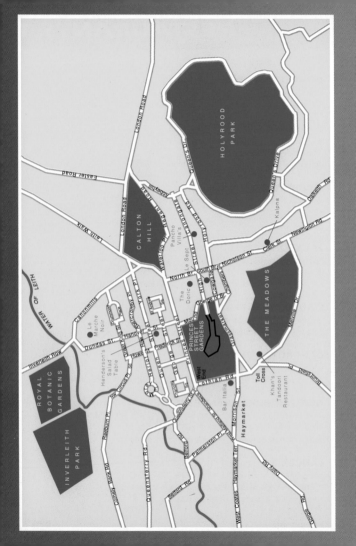

LE MARCHE NOIR 2-4 Eyre Place.
• 1200-1430, 1900-2230 Mon.-Sat. Closed Sun. • Moderate. Buses 8,19,39,23,27.
Straightforward French country-style cooking.

LE SEPT 7 Old Fishmarket Close, High St., Royal Mile.
• 1200-1430, 1830-2230 Mon.-Sat., 1830-2230 Sun. • Moderate to inexpensive. Buses 23,24,27,30,34,40,41,42,45,46,89.
Classic French cuisine, with a less expensive brasserie upstairs.

KHAN'S TANDOORI RESTAURANT 6 Brougham St., Tollcross.
• Daily 1700-0230. • Inexpensive. Buses 9,10,11,15,16,18,23,24,27.
Friendly curry house --- generous helpings of traditional Indian dishes.

BAR ITALIA 100 Lothian Road.
• Daily 1700-0230. • Inexpensive. Buses 9,10,11,15,16,18,34,35,62.
Excellent pizzas and pasta dishes, ideal for hungry late-night revellers.

PANCHO VILLA'S 240 Canongate, Royal Mile.
• 1200-1400, 1830-2230 Mon.-Fri., 1800-2300 Sat., 1900-2200 Sun.
• Moderate. Buses 1,6.
Informal atmosphere, delicious, freshly prepared Mexican food.

HENDERSON'S SALAD TABLE 94 Hanover St.
• 0800-2300 Mon.-Sat. Closed Sun. • Moderate.
Popular, self-service restaurant offering huge selection of salads.

KALPNA 2-3 St Patrick's Sq.
• 1200-1400, 1730-2330 Mon.-Sat. • Budget to moderate.
Buses 3,7,8,21,31,33, 80,82,87.
A southern Indian, non-smoking, vegetarian restaurant.

THE DORIC 5 Market St.
• 1200-0100 Mon.-Wed., 1200-0200 Thu.-Sat., 1830-2300 Sun.
• Inexpensive to moderate.
Bar and bistro serving a range of appetising dishes .

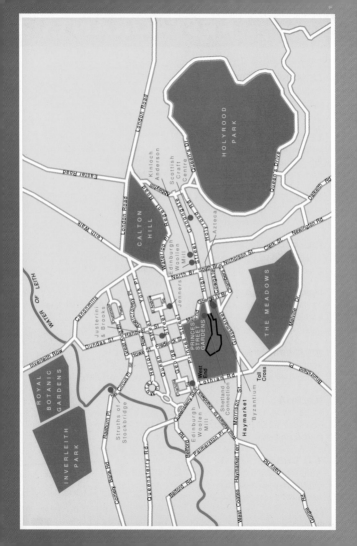

JENNERS Princes St., at corner with South St Andrews St.
•0900-1730 Mon.-Sat. (1930 on Thu.).
Quality department store offering a huge selection of goods.

KINLOCH ANDERSON 45 High St., Royal Mile.
•0900-1730 Mon.-Sat. (1700 Nov.-Mar.). Buses 3,21,31,33,34,35,80.
The best in Highland dress, with a range of over 350 authentic tartans.

EDINBURGH WOOLLEN MILL 139 Princes St. & 51 High St.
•0900-1730 Mon.-Sat. Closed Sun.
Good value range of knitwear, tweeds, gloves, hats, bags and slippers.

THE SHETLAND CONNECTION 491 Lawnmarket, Royal Mile.
•1000-2000 Sun.-Fri., 1000-2200 Sat. Buses 23, 24, 30, 35, 40, 46, 89.
Hand-made Shetland, Fair Isle and Aran knitwear. Original designs.

BYZANTIUM Victoria St.
•1000-1730 Mon.-Sat. Buses 23,24,27,30,40,41,42,45,46, 72,89.
A pleasant collection of shops selling antiques, paintings, jewellery etc.

SCOTTISH CRAFT CENTRE 140 Canongate, Royal Mile.
•1000-1730 Mon.-Sat. Buses 1,6.
Showcase for Scottish crafts, selling ceramics, pottery, textiles, jewellery.

AZTECA 16 Victoria St.
•1000-1800 Mon.-Sat.; 1000-1900 Mon.-Sat. during the Festival.
Buses 23,24,27,30,40,41,42,45,46, 72,89.
Jewellery, tapestries and ceramics imported directly from South America.

JUSTERINI & BROOKS 39 George St.
•0900-1800 Mon.-Fri.
Over 130 brands of malt whisky, along with decanters, glasses, and wines.

STRUTHS OF STOCKBRIDGE 39 Deanhaugh St., Stockbridge.
•0900-1730 Mon.-Sat. Closed Sun. Buses 24,28,29,34,35,41.
The finest haggis and prime Scottish beef and smoked salmon.

MEADOWBANK SPORTS CENTRE 139 London Rd.
• 0900-2130. • Cost based on facilities used. Bus 4, 5,15, 26, 44.
Sports centre and athletics stadium.Temporary membership available.
Facilities for athletics, fitness training, badminton, tennis, squash, cycling.

ROYAL COMMONWEALTH POOL 21 Dalkeith Rd.
• 0900-2100 Mon.-Fri., 1000-1600 Sat.-Sun. • Cost 80p for pool. Buses
2,12,21,33,82, 83.
50 m main pool, 20 m learner's pool, diving pool. Also multi-gym and
sauna, waterslides. See **CHILDREN.**

GOLF *Golf courses are plentiful -- there are 28 within the city limits and*
over 80 within 20 miles of the city centre. Most clubs welcome visitors .For
full details, contact the Tourist Centre in Waverley Market.

ANGLING *The waters around Edinburgh are well-stocked with brown*
and rainbow trout (trout season: 1 Apr.-30 Sep.), and there is fishing for
pike, perch, and roach on the Union Canal. Contact the Tourist Centre. The
booklet, Guide to Freshwater Fishing in the Lothian Region *is available free*
from Dept of Planning, Lothian Region Council, 12 St Giles St., Edinburgh.

PORT EDGAR SAILING CENTRE South Queensferry (16 km
from city). • 1000-2100 Easter-Oct. Buses: Eastern Scottish from St
Andrews Square Bus Station.
Sailboards and sailing dinghys for hire: • 2-hour sessions: sailboard £3.90;
Topper dinghy £4.50; Wayfarer dinghy £11.80.

EDINBURGH & LASSWADE RIDING CENTRE Kevock Rd,
Lasswade. Buses 80, 84. • £6 per hour inc. hire of hard hat.
Organised pony-trekking through the countryside around Edinburgh.

HILLEND SKI CENTRE Biggar Road, Fairmilehead.
• 0930-2200 Sep.-Apr.; 0930-2100 Mon.-Fri. (Sat.-Sun. 1700) May-Aug.
• Hourly, incl.equipment: Mon.-Fri. £2.90, Sat.-Sun. £3.50. Buses 4,62.
The longest artificial ski-slope in Britain. There is a chairlift and tows, and
the slope is floodlit at night. Cafeteria with bar.

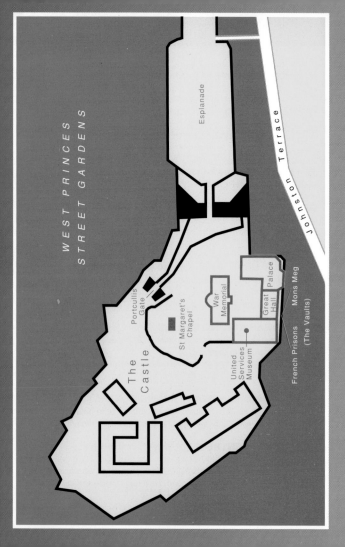

EDINBURGH CASTLE Entrance at top of Royal Mile.
•0930-1715 Mon.-Sat., 1030-1645 Sun., Apr.-Sept.; 0930-1620
Mon.-Sat.,1230-1535 Sun., Oct.-Mar. Closed Jan. 1-4. • £2.00, £1.00
child, £4.00 family. Buses 1, 6, 23, 27, 30, 34, 35, 40, 41, 42, 46, 89.

ESPLANADE & GATEHOUSE *The Esplanade (built in 1753) is the
setting for the Military Tattoo.The Gatehouse is Victorian, built 1882-88. The
statues are of Robert the Bruce and William Wallace.*

PORTCULLIS GATE & MILLS MOUNT BATTERY *The gate
stands on site of 14thC Constable's Tower, and dates from 1577, rebuilt in
1867. The Battery overlooks Princes St., and it is from here that the one
o'clock gun is fired each day.*

ST MARGARET'S CHAPEL *The city's oldest surviving building, dating from the 12thC, occupies the highest point of the Castle Rock. It was
built by David I, son of the saintly Queen Margaret, in 1097.*

SCOTTISH UNITED SERVICES MUSEUM
•0930-1230, 1400-1700 Mon.-Sat., 1230-1630 Sun. •Free.
Covers the history of the armed forces in Scotland.

THE GREAT HALL *Splendid hall, built at the order of James IV in the
16thC, sits on top of the French Prisons. There is fine wood-panelling, displays of weapons and armour, and an impressive hammer-beam roof.*

THE FRENCH PRISONS *These gloomy dungeons, deep in the vaults
below the Great Hall, held French prisoners during the Napoleonic Wars.
Graffiti written by the unfortunate inmates can still be seen on the walls.*

MONS MEG *A magnificent siege cannon dating from c.1440, and once
capable of firing 150 kg cannonballs at targets up to 1600 m away.*

THE PALACE *This 16thC Palace was the royal residence before the
completion of Holyroodhouse at the far end of the Royal Mile. It is now the
home of the Scottish Regalia - Crown, Sword and Sceptre.*

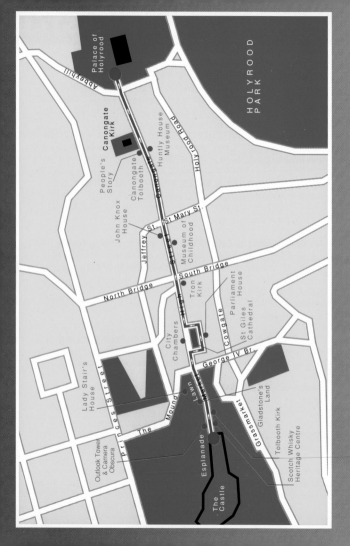

The Royal Mile

Time required: 2 to 4 hours.

This historic thoroughfare links two of the city's main tourist attractions, the Castle and Holyroodhouse. There is much to see. The time required will depend on how many stops you make to visit the various museums and buildings.

Begin at the Castle Esplanade. On the right is 'Cannonball House' (built 1630). The cannonball lodged in the wall was not fired in anger, but marks the gravitation height of the city's first piped water supply. Across the street is a fountain (dated 1722) which marks the spot where hundreds of women were burnt as witches. At the corner with Ramsay Lane is the **Outlook Tower & Camera Obscura**, while on the right is the **Scotch Whisky Heritage Centre**. As you descend Castlehill, the Tolbooth Kirk (1842-44) comes into view -- its 240ft spire is the tallest in Edinburgh. (*20 min.*).

A few yards beyond the kirk, on the left, is **Gladstone's Land**, and through the neighbouring close you will find **Lady Stair's House.** Cross George IV Bridge (a brass plaque in the roadway on the right-hand side marks the site of the city's last public execution in 1864), and go right into Parliament Square. Brass plaques in the cobblestones in front of **St Giles Cathedral** mark the outline of the Tolbooth (old town gaol, demolished in 1817), while the **Heart of Midlothian** marks the site of the condemned cell. After visiting the **Parliament House & Law Courts**, leave the square at the Mercat Cross (includes part of original 15thC cross), opposite the splendid City Chambers (John Adam, 1761). At the downhill end of the Chambers is Anchor Close, where in 1768 William Smellie printed the first edition of the Encyclopaedia Britannica. On the junction with South Bridge stands the Tron Kirk, which dates from 1637 (named after the tron, or weighing machine, that once stood on the spot). (*40 min.*).

Beyond the Bridges, on the left is Paisley Close, with an inscription above the entrance which reads *Heave awa' chaps, I'm no' deid yet*, the words of a man who was rescued from a tenement collapse here in 1861. Downhill on the right is the **Museum of Childhood**, and where the street narrows is the distinctive **John Knox House**. At the junction with St Mary's St. and Jeffrey St. more brass plaques mark the outline of the old Netherbow Port (built 1513, demolished 1764), one of the six

gates in the old city wall. Its original appearance can be seen in a model on display in **Huntly House Museum**. (*40 min.*).

Continue down the Canongate, passing on the right Chessel's Court, where Deacon Brodie was caught robbing the Excise Office and was subsequently hanged. Further down is **Huntly House Museum,** and across the street, the **Canongate Tolbooth** and the museum illustrating the history of the local people: **The People's Story**. Next to the Tolbooth is Canongate Kirk (1688). The surrounding kirkyard contains the graves of Adam Smith, the economist, and the poet Robert Fergusson. Fergusson's headstone was erected by Robert Burns, and later renovated by R.L. Stevenson. Near the foot of the Canongate, on the left, is White Horse Close, a converted 17thC coaching inn which was once the departure point for the stagecoach to London. (*30 min.*).

Cross the roundabout to Abbey Strand, and finish your walk at the gates of Holyroodhouse, erected in 1922 as part of a memorial to King Edward VII.

75

e CurioS

363

361

C

CA

WE BUY
ANTIQUE
JEWELLERY

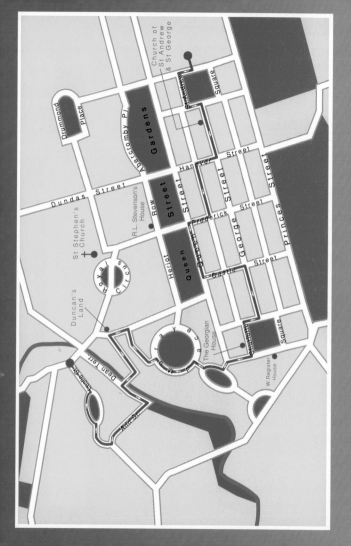

The New Town

Time required: 1-1/2 to 2 hours. Begin in St Andrew Sq., in front of the Royal Bank of Scotland building, built in 1772-74 as a house for Sir Lawrence Dundas. Go around the north side, which has some of the New Town's earliest houses (*eg* no.26, built about 1722), and go along George St. On the right is the church of St Andrew and St George (1782), with an interesting oval interior. Go right into Hanover St then left along Thistle St. This and Rose St. were built to house the humbler folk of the New Town. Today Thistle St is lined by bistros, coffee-houses and antique shops. Turn right down Frederick St., with a view of St Stephen's Church (William Playfair, 1828), one of the New Town's most distinctive landmarks. (*20 min.*).

Left to Queen St., with its private gardens (1823). The lake and island in these gardens are said to have been the inspiration for R.L. Stevenson's *Treasure Island*; the author lived in Heriot Row, across the gardens. Left up Castle St. (no.39 was the home of Sir Walter Scott from 1802-26), right into George St. and right again to Charlotte Sq., and go around the north side, whose magnificent facade was designed by Robert Adam, with modifications by Robert Reid. It was built in 1792-1805. No.5, headquarters of the National Trust for Scotland, no.6 office of the Secretary of State for Scotland, and no.7 the restored Georgian House museum (see **MUSEUMS**). The dome on the west side belongs to West Register House, originally St George's Church. Alexander Graham Bell, inventor of the telephone, lived in a house at the corner of the square and S Charlotte St. (*20 min.*).

Leave the square by Glenfinlas St. Ainslie Pl., along with Randolph Cres. and Moray Pl., forms the Moray Estate, an impressive develop-ment built 1822-27. Go through Great Stuart St. and round Moray Pl., left at Doune Terr. (views of Stockbridge and Fettes College), and left again down Gloucester St. to Duncan's Land, built as a house about 1746 (the lintel dated 1605 was brought from a house in the Old Town) but now a restaurant. (*15 min.*).

Left into India Pl., right over the Water of Leith (see **WALK 4**), then left up Dean Terr. and right into Ann St, built 1816-27 for Sir Henry Raeburn and named after his wife. At the far end, go right into Dean Park Cres. and on to St Bernard's Cres. (built 1824) with its Doric columns. Left into Leslie Pl. to finish in Stockbridge (see **CITY DISTRICTS**). (*20 min.*).

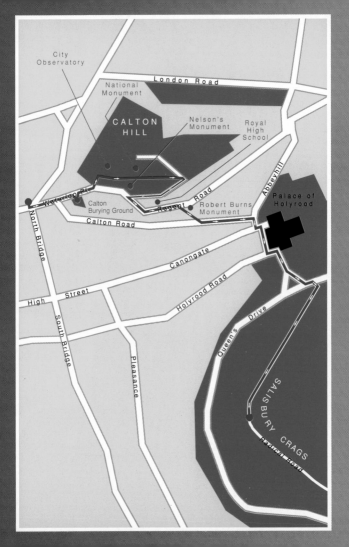

Calton Hill

Time required: 2 to 3 hours. Begin at the east end of Princes St., in front of the impressive Register House, designed by Robert Adam and built 1774-88. This is the place where those hoping to trace their Scots ancestry begin their search. Head into Waterloo Pl. and cross Waterloo Bridge with its memorial arches and dramatic views. On the right is the Calton Burying Ground with its obelisk commemorating Australia's political martyrs of 1793 and the graves of many of Edinburgh's prominent citizens. Cross the street to a flight of stairs, climb up these then right up a path to the top of Calton Hill. (*30 min.*).

The summit of Calton Hill bristles with monuments, and helped to earn Edinburgh the title 'Athens of the North'. The most impressive is the unfinished National Monument, with its twelve columns. It was begun in the early 1820s as a memorial to the dead of the Napoleonic Wars, but funds ran out and it was never completed. The 30 m/100 ft high Nelson Monument (built 1807) is today used as a private residence, but you can climb the steps to the top for superb views (50p). Nearby are Dugald Stewart's Monument (1831) and the City Observatory (1818), both designed by William Playfair. Descend by the path beyond the Nelson Monument, and exit onto Regent Rd. (*30 min.*).

To the right is St Andrew's House (Government offices). Cross the road to enjoy views over the Old Town and Arthur's Seat, then head left along Regent Rd. On the left above the road is the Greek Doric edifice of the former Royal High School (built 1825-29) and on the right is a monument to Robert Burns, built in 1830. Retrace your steps for a few yards and go through the gate on the left and descend the path leading down to Calton Rd. Walk left along this road to reach the foot of the Royal Mile. (*20 min.*).

The last part of this walk is for those still feeling energetic, and good walking shoes are recommended. Go along Horse Wynd and turn left into Holyrood Park. Salisbury Crags tower above, fading into the hillside. Where the rocks end there is a flight of stairs: climb these, then turn right and climb up the steep track. This path goes all the way along the foot of the crags, and is known as the Radical Road. The views from here are superb, ranging from the Pentland Hills to the destinctive skyline of the Old Town and the County of Fife, lying over the Firth of Forth. (*30 min.*).

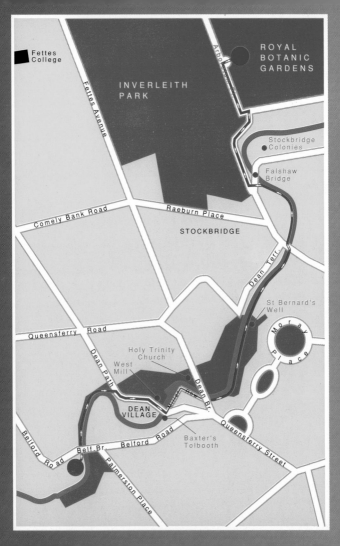

Fettes College

ROYAL BOTANIC GARDENS

INVERLEITH PARK

Fettes Avenue

Arbo...

Stockbridge Colonies

Falshaw Bridge

Comely Bank Road

Raeburn Place

STOCKBRIDGE

Dean Terr.

St Bernard's Well

Queensferry Road

Dean Path

Moray Place

Holy Trinity Church

West Mill

Dean Br.

DEAN VILLAGE

Belford Road

Belf. Br.

Belford Road

Baxter's Tolbooth

Queensferry Street

Palmerston Place

Water of Leith

Time required: about 1 hour. Begin at the Hilton National Hotel, Belford Rd (buses: LRT 41 to Dean Bridge, then walk along Belford Rd. Eastern Scottish C13 to hotel). Go down the road named Bells Mills to reach the walkway on the bank of the river. The Water of Leith rises in the Pentland Hills and flows 37 km to the sea at Leith, its deep, wooded valley cutting a leafy swathe through the city. Go left passing under Belford Bridge (built 1885-87). Beyond the bridge the path passes through woods before climbing a flight of steps to Dean Path. Go right down the hill into the picturesque Dean Village (see **CITY DISTRICTS**). The Incorporation of Baxters (Bakers' Union) once managed 11 mills and 2 granaries here. To the left of the bridge is the huge West Mill, rebuilt in 1805, and now converted to flats. It is the city's largest surviving industrial building of that era. High above the river is the spire of Holy Trinity Church. *(20 min.)*

Cross the bridge to Baxter's Tolbooth on the right. A carved stone over the door shows bakers' shovels with three loaves, and the words *God Bless the Baxters of Edinburgh who built this house in 1675*. Across the road on the parapet of the bridge are more carved stones. The steep hill leading up from the bridge, Bells Brae, was once the main road out of Edinburgh, heading to Queensferry. Go left down Miller Row. On the left beside the weir is the site of Lindsay's Mill, of which three millstones remain as a monument in the little park beyond. Continue under the soaring arches of the Dean Bridge, built by Thomas Telford in 1832. It is 32m/106ft high. The path now passes beneath the private Moray Bank Pl. Gardens, to reach St Bernard's Well. This was built in 1789 and was once a popular mineral spring; the statue is of Hygeia, goddess of health. Go down the stairs at the well and follow the riverside path under St Bernard's Bridge and on to Stockbridge. *(20 min.)*

Cross the bridge to the left and descend the stairs on far side to continuation of walkway, and follow this to Falshaw Bridge. Bear left across the road, and go right into Arboretum Ave. On the left are playing fields, with the Gothic spires of Fettes College beyond. The neat terraced houses across the river to the right are the Stockbridge Colonies, a 19thC development built by an artisan's co-operative to provide affordable housing for tradesmen. Continue along Arboretum Pl. to end your walk at the entrance to the **Royal Botanic Garden**. *(20 min.)*

Accidents and Breakdowns: If you are involved in an accident where no-one has been hurt, exchange your name, address and insurance details with the other driver. If there are any injuries the police must be notified, and an ambulance called.

In the event of a breakdown, AA and RAC members can call 24-hour breakdown service: AA (031) 220 1999; RAC (031) 228 3911. Garages providing a 24 hour breakdown service include: P. Barlas Garage Services (031) 669 6867; Lochend Motor Co. (031) 661 6264 day/554 6558 night.

Edinburgh offices of motoring organisations: Automobile Association, 18-22 Melville St., tel: (031) 226 4031; Royal Automobile Club, 17 Rutland Sq., tel: (031) 229 2500.

Accommodation: Edinburgh offers a wide range of accommodation, from the humble bed and breakfast to the world-class luxury hotel. The STB has recently introduced a two-tier system of classifying hotels and guest-houses: the range of facilities available is indicated by the 'Classification', ranging from 1-crown for basic accommodation to 5-crowns for a luxury suite; and the quality of service is shown by the grading, which can be 'Approved', 'Commended' or 'Highly Commended'. Room prices must, by law, be prominently displayed. Range of prices for double room with breakfast: guest house £8 - 20; hotel £18 - 65 and over.

A list of hotels (*Tourist Accommodation Register*) is available free from the Tourist Information & Accommodation Centre at Waverley Market. The Tourist Centre also provides a year-round Advance Reservation Service (at least 3 weeks notice required), and an On-The-Spot Reservation Service during peak summer months. There are other Accommodation Centres at Waverley Station and Edinburgh Airport. You are strongly advised not to arrive in Edinburgh during the Festival without having booked your accommodation well in advance.

Airport: Edinburgh Airport lies 10 km west of the city, on the main A8 road to Glasgow. A regular 'Airporter' bus service runs between the terminal and Waverley Bridge in the city centre (from 0600-2230; service every 30 mins 0820-1610, less frequent at week ends; journey time

approx. 30 mins; cost £1.75 single, £3.00 day-return). A taxi from airport to city centre costs about £7. Airport facilities include Tourist Information & Accommodation Desk (tel: (031) 333 2167), bank, currency exchange, restaurant, buffet, 2 bars, duty-free shop, gift-shop, qualified nurse, facilities for disabled travellers. Enquiries: tel (031) 333 1000 and ask for Airport Information Desk.

Arthur's Seat: A familiar Edinburgh landmark, this craggy hill rises above Holyroodhouse to a height of 251 m/823 ft. A walk to its summit will be rewarded with panoramic views over the city. It was named in the 15thC during a revival of interest in Arthurian romances.

Baby Sitters: Available from Bruntsfield Helping Hands Agency, 45 Barclay Place, tel: (031) 228 1382 or 2858. Many of the better hotels will provide a baby-sitting service.

Banks: see **Money**.

Best Buys: Edinburgh abounds with shops selling good quality Scottish goods. The most popular souvenirs include fine woollen

knitwear, hand-woven tweed from the Hebrides, and, of course, kilts and tartan skirts. Scottish crafts, such as pottery, ceramics and silver jewellery, are often good value. Traditional Scottish produce like smoked salmon and haggis can be deliverd by mail order all over the world, while a tin of shortbread or a packet of oatcakes will not take up much room in your suitcase. And don't forget to take home a bottle or two of fine malt whisky!

Budget: Accommodation: double room with bath and breakfast in hotel, £30-75; double room without bath in B & B, £8-18.
Lunch for two in cafe or pub: £5-16.
Dinner for two, without wine, in restaurant: £12-40.
Drinks in pub: pint of beer about £1.04, whisky about 85p.
Museum admission: mostly free.

Burke and Hare: William Burke and William Hare were notorious murderers who once prowled the streets and closes of Edinburgh's Old Town. In 1827 they strangled at least 16 people and sold the corpses to surgeons for medical research. Hare finally confessed to the horrific crimes, and testified against Burke in a sensational trial. Burke was hanged in the Grassmarket on 28 January, 1829, and his own corpse was subsequently dissected. His skeleton remains to this day in Edinburgh University's Department of Anatomy.

Burns, Robert: The poet Robert Burns (1759 -96) is known and loved the world over through such classics as '*Tam O'Shanter*', '*My Love Is Like A Red, Red Rose*', and '*Auld Lang Syne*'. Born in Alloway in Ayrshire, Burns first came to Edinburgh in 1768 to make his name in the Scottish capital, which he did - the Edinburgh edition of his poems sold 3000 copies. On a later visit he fell in love with Mrs Agnes Maclehose (the 'Clarinda' of his poems), who inspired the moving love-song, *Ae Fond Kiss*. She is buried in the Canongate Kirkyard. His last visit to the city was in 1791, when he lodged at the White Hart Inn in the Grassmarket. There is a monument to Burns on Regent Road, and relics associated with the poet can be seen in Lady Stair's House Museum (see **AZ**).

Bus & Coach Services: The main city bus network is run by Lothian Region Transport (LRT), Head Office at 14 Queen St., tel: (031) 554 4494. Enquiries, maps and timetables: Ticket Centre, 5 Waverley Bridge, tel: 226 5087. Their maroon-and-white buses cover most of the city. Most services leave from Princes St.: each bus-stop shows the numbers of the bus services that halt there. Pay your fare to the driver as you board; carry plenty of small change, as only the exact fare is accepted (20-90p depending on journey; tell driver your destination and he will tell you how much to pay; children under 5 travel free). Special tourist tickets giving unlimited bus travel for 1 to 13 days are available from the Ticket Centre. Between 30 May and 2 Sep a special Tourist Shuttle (service 99) runs every 30mins Mon-Fri from Princes St., passing most major tourist attractions (flat fare 75p adult, 40p child). The green-and-white buses of Eastern Scottish Omnibuses (St Andrews Square Bus Station, tel: (031) 556 8464) serve the towns and villages around Edinburgh, and also cover a number of city routes.
Scottish Citylink (St Andrews Square Bus Station, tel: (031) 557 5717) run blue-and-yellow coaches providing long-distance and inter-city ser-vices throughout Scotland and the UK, *eg* Edinburgh to Glasgow, 70

mins, £3.40 return; Edinburgh to London, 9hrs, £25.00 return. For the London service it is advisable to book a seat in advance.

Calton Hill: The rocky hill rising to 100 m/328 ft at the east end of Princes St. Its summit is crowned with a number of interesting monuments. See **WALK 3.**

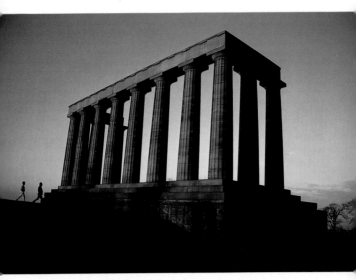

Camping and Caravaning: The booklet *Scotland: Caravan and Camping Sites* is available from STB and BTA offices. Two sites serving the city are: Drum Mohr Caravan Park, Levenhall, Musselburgh (to east of city), tel: (031) 665 6867, open Mar.-Oct., cost of pitch (caravan, motor-caravan or tent): £5.00/night for 2 people (£5.50 in Jul. & Aug.), plus 50p for each extra person, electricity hook-up, £1.00 extra;

Mortonhall Caravan Park, 30 Frogston Road East (south of city), tel: (031) 664 1533. Open Mar 28-Oct 31, Cost of pitch (caravan, motor-caravan or tent): £7.50/night; electricity hook-up, £1.25 extra; awning £1.75 extra.

Car Hire: Most car hire companies require that you be over 21, with at least 12 months experience on a full licence. A cash deposit will be needed unless you are paying by credit card. Rates and systems of charging vary from company to company, so make sure you are aware of the full cost inclusive of insurance, VAT and any surcharges. Third party insurance is compulsory; collision damage insurance is optional, but recommended.
Avis: Edinburgh Airport (031) 333 1866; 100 Dalry Rd (031) 337 6363.
Budget: 116 Polwarth Gdns (031) 228 6088.
Godfrey Davis: Edinburgh Airport (031) 333 2588; 24 East London St (031) 661 1252.
Hertz: Edinburgh Airport (031) 333 1019; Waverley Station Rail-Drive (031) 556 8835; 10 Picardy Place (031) 556 8311.
Other firms can be found in the Yellow Pages telephone directory.

Charlotte Square: see WALK 2

Canongate Tolbooth: see WALK 1

Chemists: see Pharmacies

Children: Edinburgh offers many activities for children, from building sandcastles on Portobello Beach, to flying kites in Holyrood Park. See **CHILDREN**. There is an informative booklet *Scotland For Children* available from the STB. You should be aware that children are not generally welcome in pubs in the city, though some country inns may advertise 'family rooms'.

Cigarettes and Tobacco: Widely available in tobacconists, newsagents, grocers shops, cafes and pubs. Cost about £1.75 for a packet of 20 cigarettes. Look out for no-smoking areas in buses, trains and some restaurants. Note that British Airways has banned smoking completely on all domestic flights. There is a specialist tobacconist shop at Herbert Love, 31 Queensferry St, selling quality tobacco, cigars, pipes, lighters, humidors and other smoking accessories.

Climate: Edinburgh enjoys a much drier but much colder climate than Glasgow and the west of Scotland. The best months to visit are May and June, when it is least likely to rain, and many flowers and trees are in full bloom. Average temperatures and rainfall: 4° C in winter, 2.7 in. of rain: 7° C in spring, 2.2 in. of rain; 15° C in summer, 2.7 in. of rain; and 7° C in autumn, 3.1 in. of rain.

Consulates: American Consulate General, 3 Regent Terrace, Edinburgh, tel: (031) 556 8315. Australian Consulate, Hobart House, 80 Hanover St, Edinburgh, tel: (031) 226 6271. Canadian Consulate, 195 West George St, Glasgow, tel: (041) 248 3026. South African Consulate, 69 Nelson Mandela Place, Glasgow, tel: (041) 221 3114.

Conversion Charts:

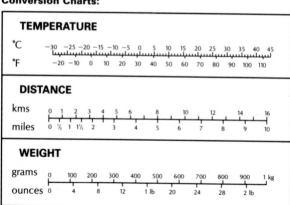

Credit Cards; see **Money.**

Crime & Theft: Crime in Edinburgh is low compared to many other capital cities, but you should still take precautions. Keep your valuables in the hotel safe; take special care of your wallet or handbag in crowded streets or shops; always lock your car, and leave anything of value, such as a camera, out of sight in the boot.

Currency: The British unit of currency is the pound (£), equal to 100 pence (p). Banknotes come in denominations of £50 (red), £20 (purple), £10 (brown), £5 (blue) and £1 (green). The coins are £1, 50p, 20p, 10p, 5p, 2p and 1p. Note that the three Scottish banks (Bank of Scotland, Royal Bank and Clydesdale Bank) all issue their own distinctive banknotes, which are different in appearance (but not in value) from their English equivalents - the one-pound coin. English £1 notes are no longer in circulation.

Customs:

Duty Paid Into:	Cigarettes	or	Cigars	or	Tobacco	Spirits	Wine
E.E.C.	300		75		400 g	1.5 *l*	5 *l*
U.K.	300		75		400 g	1.5 *l*	5 *l*

Deacon Brodie: 18thC city councillor Deacon William Brodie was, by day, a well-respected businessman. But at night he lived a secret life as a gambler, rogue and burglar, stealing to support his gambling debts, two mistresses and five illegitimate children. He was finally caught in the act of robbing the Excise Office in Chessel's Court, Canongate (see **WALK 1**), and was hanged at the the Tolbooth on 1 October, 1788, in front of a crowd of 40,000. His double life is said to have been the inspiration behind R.L.Stevenson's story of *Dr Jekyll and Mr Hyde.*

Dentists: see **Health.**

Disabled: Many places in Edinburgh have facilities for disabled visitors. For details, contact the Tourist Centre, Waverley Market.

Drinks: Scotland is world-famous for its whisky (the name comes from the Gaelic *uisge-beatha*, meaning 'water of life'). There are over 2000 brands of whisky to choose from. Over a hundred of these are single malts, distilled purely from malted barley and aged in wooden

casks, each as distinctive to the experienced palate as a classic wine. The rest are blends, mixtures of 15 to 50 grain whiskies (distilled from a mix of malted barley with other, unmalted cereals), with a smaller amount of malt whiskies.

The breweries in and around Edinburgh produce some excellent beers. Names to look out for include Belhaven, Maclay's, Caledonian,

Greenmantle and McEwan's 80/-. Beers are often classified in the traditional manner, as 60/-, 70/- or 80/- in order of increasing strength. These are roughly equivalent to English mild, bitter and best. Among non-alcoholic drinks, mineral water is becoming increasingly popular, and in addition to the usual French brands there are some Scottish waters, such as Highland Spring.

Driving: You will need your driving licence (foreign licences can be used in the UK for up to 12 months), and registration and insurance documents if you are bringing your own vehicle. Driving is on the left side of the road. The wearing of seat-belts is compulsory for the driver and front-seat passenger, and recommended for back-seat passengers. Road regulations are detailed in the booklet *The Highway Code*, available from the AA, RAC and many bookshops. Most road signs conform to international standards. Speed limits are 30 or 40 mph/48 or 64 kph in built-up areas, 60 mph/96 kph on single-carriageway main roads, and 70 mph/112 kph on dual carriageways and motorways. Driving conditions are generally good.

Driving in the city centre can be frustrating because of congestion,

especially during the peak hours 0800-0900 and 1700-1800. The left-hand lane of many main streets is marked off by a solid white line. This lane is reserved for the use of buses only, between the hours of 0830-0915 and 1640-1800.

There are city centre car-parks at Castle Terrace (off Lothian Road) and the St James's Centre (east end of Princes St). There are parking meters on many streets (20mins for 10p). A single yellow line at the kerb means no parking during daytime; a double yellow line means no parking at any time. Traffic wardens are plentiful and vigilant. Penalties for illegal parking range from a £12 fine to the towing away and impounding of the vehicle.

Petrol is widely available from service stations throughout the city, unleaded petrol is indicated by a green sign. Many stations are self-service. 24-hour petrol station: Links Service Station, 21-27 Barclay Place, Tollcross, also has a 24-hour grocery department.

Eating Out: Edinburgh offers a wide range of cuisine, from traditional Scottish fare, through classic French, Italian and Chinese cooking, to Mexican, Thai, Armenian and even Peruvian food. Many restaurants are concentrated in the city centre, especially in the New Town and in the streets and closes along the Royal Mile. Many less expensive eating places can be found along Lothian Road and in the Tollcross area, and outlets for fast-food - pizza, kebabs, hamburgers and the traditional fish and chips - are widely distributed. Lunch is generally served 1200-1400, and dinner 1900-2200. Some smaller Chinese and Indian restaurants serve food all day and stay open until after midnight, and a few Italian places in Lothian Road stay open until 3am or 4am. *The Scotsman* and *Evening News* newspapers contain useful lists of restaurants. Expect to pay around £7-16 per head for an average three-course meal without wine.

Edinburgh Castle: Perched on its volcanic crag, Edinburgh's castle dominates the city below. There has been a fortification on the Castle Rock since at least the 6thC, but the first proper fortress and royal residence were built in the 11thC for Malcolm Canmore, and his Saxon queen, Margaret. Her son, David I, is thought to have built St

Margaret's Chapel, the oldest surviving building on the Rock (and in the city), when he moved the Scottish capital from Dunfermline to Edinburgh in 1124. Since that time, the Castle has been added to gradually over the centuries, attaining its present form around the beginning of the 20thC. The Castle's last active role in military conflict was in 1745, during the Jacobite uprising. Today its military links remain strong: it is the Regimental HQ of the Royal Scots and Royal Scots Dragoon Guards, the home of the Army School of Piping, and the setting for the famous, annual Military Tattoo. See **CASTLE**.

Edinburgh Crystal Visitor's Centre: Eastfield, Penicuik, Midlothian (16 km south of the city), tel: (0968) 75128 or 72244. Here you can watch the production of fine crystal glassware, including glass-blowing, cooling, cutting, polishing and engraving. Guided tours of the Works: 0915-1530 Mon.-Fri. Cost £1.00, 50p child 10-16 yrs (for safety

reasons, no children under 10 allowed on tours). Also large factory shop selling glassware and tableware, open 0900-1700 Mon.-Sat. (1000-1700 Sun. Apr.-Sep.). Closed Dec. 25-Jan 6.

Edinburgh International Festival; The world's largest arts festival is held for three weeks every August, when the city's population is doubled with the arrival of over 500,000 visitors and performers. From its beginnings in 1947 the festival has grown in stature, and produced many offshoots, notably the Festival Fringe (see **Fringe**), and the Jazz, Film and Book Fesivals. The Military Tattoo, though not an official part of the main Festival, is held at the same time.

Information: postal enquiries to Edinburgh Festival Society, 21 Market St, Edinburgh EH1 1BW. Tel: (031) 226 4001. Programmes and ticket order forms are available from April onwards. During the Festival there is an Information Centre in front of the National Gallery on The Mound, with up-to-the-minute information on ticket availabilty, open daily 1000-1800.

Edinburgh Zoo: Founded in 1913, the Zoo occupies a pleasant 30 hectare site on Corstorphine Hill. It has over 2000 animals, including pygmy hippos, gorillas, snowy owls, and a pair of rare snow leopards. It is famous for its colony of penguins, which go on a 'Penguin Parade' 1430 daily, Apr.-Sep. Another popular attraction is sea-lion feeding-time at 1500 daily. Facilities include a Children's Farm, Adventure Playground, restaurant, bookshop and picnic areas. There are also magnificent views from the top of the hill.

Electricity: Standard voltage is 240V/50Hz AC. Adaptors will be necessary for foreign appliances. Shaver sockets are international standard 2-pin design, 240V.

Emergencies: Police, Fire Brigade or Ambulance: dial 999. On a pay-phone you can dial 999 without inserting any money. See **Crime & Theft, Health, Lost Property, Police.**

Events: Full details of events in the city are available from the Tourist Centre at Waverley Market.
25 January: Burns Night (dinners and parties celebrating the anniversary of the birth of Scotalnd's best-known poet).
January-March: International Rugby Union at Murrayfield Stadium.
April: Edinburgh Festival of Science & Technology; Edinburgh Folk Music Festival.
May-September: Highland Games take place all over Scotland.
June: Royal Highland Agricultural Show at Ingliston Showground.
August:: Edinburgh International Festival; Festival Fringe; Film Festival; Jazz Festival; Book Festival (biennial, next due 1989, 1991); Military Tattoo.
31 December: Hogmanay (New Year celebrations, crowds gather around Tron Kirk to bring in the New Year).

Firth of Forth: The estuary of the River Forth, a long, narrow arm of the sea that cuts into the Scottish coast immediately to the north of the city. Views to the north from George St or the Castle show the Firth with the hills of Fife beyond.

Food: Visitors to Edinburgh can look forward to sampling the full range of Scotland's natural produce: prime beef from the Aberdeen Angus herds, game and venison from the hills and moors, salmon and trout from the lochs and rivers, and of course the rich harvest of the sea: lobster, prawns, crab, oysters, herring, haddock and cod. Traditional soups include *Cock-a-leekie* (a broth of chicken, onion and leek), *Partan Bree* (a creamy crab soup), and *Cullen Skink* (made with smoked haddock, milk, onion and potato). *Loch Fyne kippers* (smoked herring) are a popular breakfast dish, or you could try an *Arbroath Smokie* (haddock smoked over birch/oak twigs) or *Finnan Haddie* (haddock smoked over peat). Scottish salmon is famed worldwide for its quality and flavour, and is equally delicious poached, baked or smoked. A main course of beef, lamb, or venison might be followed by a dessert based on Scottish fruit (e.g. raspberries, gooseberries or rhubarb), or a dish of *Athol Brose*, a rich blend of cream, whisky and oatmeal. Inexpensive pub snacks include Forfar Bridies (pastry parcels filled with minced meat and vegetables) or stovies (a filling hash of potatoes, onions, cabbage and meat). And of course there is haggis. This famous Scottish dish is prepared using the minced liver, heart and lungs of a sheep, mixed with oatmeal, onion, suet and seasoning. The mixture is used to stuff a sheep's stomach-bag, which is then sewn up and cooked either by boiling or roasting. It tastes much better than it sounds! Haggis is traditionally served with 'bashed neeps and chappit tatties' (mashed turnip and potato), and eaten on Burns' Night (25 Jan.), St Andrew's Day (30 Nov.) and Hogmanay (31 Dec.).

Forth Bridges: Two famous and spectacular bridges span the Firth of Forth at Queensferry, to the west of Edinburgh. The Forth Railway Bridge was built between 1882 and 1890, its three double-cantilevers spanning one-and-a-half miles. The Forth Road Bridge is an elegant suspension bridge, opened in 1964, and replaced the ferries which had run between North and South Queensferry since the 12thC.

Fringe: This famous offshoot of the International Festival had its origins in eight small theatre companies that were excluded from the first official Festival in 1947. They went ahead and staged their productions anyway, and began a tradition which has blossomed into an annual extravaganza of nearly 1000 shows in 130 venues, selling 470,000 tickets. None of the performers are invited. They simply apply for a venue, turn up, and do their own thing. The Fringe offers something for everyone, from theatre, comedy, cabaret and revue, to mime, dance, classical music, exhibitions, children's shows, opera, jazz, poetry, performance art, rock music and street entertainment. Information: postal enquiries to The Fringe Office, 180 High St, Edinburgh EH1 1QS. Tel: (031) 226 5257. Programmes and ticket order forms are usually available from early July onward. During the Fringe, an Information Desk will be found in the Fringe Office, 180 High St, Royal Mile, open daily 1000-1800. The Fringe Daily Diary is a free list of all Fringe events taking place on a particular day, and is available from tourist centres, hotels, venues *etc.*

Grassmarket: A wide street in the Old Town, south of the Castle, where weekly markets were held until 1911. It was once the setting for public executions: the site of the gallows is marked by a cross in the cobblestones in the small garden at the east end. The 18thC White Hart Inn, on the north side, was frequented by Highland drovers who brought their cattle here to market, and was visited by Robert Burns and William Wordsworth. The narrow vennel leading off the west end of the Grassmarket contains one of the last remnants of the old city wall, built after Scotland's defeat by the English at the Battle of Flodden in 1513.

Greyfriars Bobby: Bobby was a terrier belonging to Jock Gray, a local shepherd. When Jock died in 1858, the dog stayed faithfully at his master's graveside in Greyfriars Kirkyard, every day for 14 years. He left only to be fed at a nearby inn each day, at the sound of the one o'clock gun, and became so popular that a bronze statue of him was erected in 1873, after his death. The statue stands opposite the gates of Greyfriars Kirkyard, on the corner of George IV Bridge and Candlemaker Row. Bobby's own gravestone can be seen just inside the kirkyard gates, and his collar and bowl are on display in Huntly House Museum.

Hairdressers: There are many salons throughout the city. Expect to pay about £6 to £10. One of Edinburgh's top hairdressers is Charlie Miller, 13 Stafford St, tel: (031) 226 5550, open 0900-1700 Tue.-Sat., closed Sun.-Mon. Small gents' barber-shops will give a basic haircut for £2 to £3.

Haymarket: Edinburgh's second main-line railway station. It is not a terminus, merely a stop on the main line west to Glasgow and London Euston, 4 minutes from Edinburgh Waverley. It is more convenient for people staying in the West End of the city.

Health: Overseas visitors are eligible for free emergency treatment under Britain's National Health Service, at hospital Accident & Emergency Departments, but you are strongly recommended to take out adequate medical insurance before your trip. EC nationals can take advantage of reciprocal health care arrangements by filling out form E111 before their trip. Contact your own Health Service for details.
In a medical emergency, dial 999 and ask for an ambulance. There are 24 hour Accident & Emergency Depts at the Royal Infirmary, Lauriston Place (tel: (031) 229 2477), and the Western General Hospital, Crewe Road South (tel: (031) 332 2525).
For less serious complaints, make an appointment to see a local doctor. Your hotel, or the local police station, will have a list of available doctors.
For emergency dental treatment, contact the Edinburgh Dental Hospital, 31 Chambers St, tel: (031) 225 9511.

Heart of Midlothian: On the south side of the Royal Mile, just to the west of St Giles Cathedral, this heart-shaped pattern of cobblestones set into the road marks the site of the Old Tolbooth, once the notorious town prison. It was demolished in 1817, but brass plates in the road mark its original outline. The old custom of spitting on the Heart for good luck persists to the present day.

Holyroodhouse, Palace of: The Palace is the Royal Family's official Scottish residence. It was founded in the late 15thC by James IV,

and probably had its origins in the guest-quarters attached to the neighbouring 12thC Abbey of Holyrood (the abbey ruins lie behind the present-day palace). The Palace, which was extensively re-built and expanded in the 17thC, has close links with Mary, Queen of Scots, who lived there from 1564 to 1570, through the troubled years of the murder of her secretary Rizzio in 1556, and the death of her husband Lord Darnley in 1567. Rizzio was stabbed to death in one of Mary's rooms by her jealous husband and his accomplices; a brass plaque in the floor marks the spot where he fell. Bonnie Prince Charlie stayed here during the '45, and George IV used the Palace during his historic visit in 1822. It was at King George's behest that the Palace was refurbished, and renovation and restoration continued over the next hundred years. Most of the Palace is open to public view (except when the Queen is in residence), including the Throne Room, Drawing Rooms, the sumptuous King's Bedchamber, the Picture Gallery, and Lord Darnley's and Mary's Rooms. Guided tours only, 0930-1715, Mon.-Sat., 1030-1630 Sun. Apr.-Sep.; 0930-1545 Mon.-Sat. Oct-Mar. Tours start every 15mins in summer and last 35mins. £1.60, 80p child.

Insurance: Overseas visitors are strongly recommended to take out

medical and travel insurance before departing for the UK. Your travel agent will be able to recommend a suitable policy.

John Knox House: 45 High St, Royal Mile. This interesting house dates from the early 16thC, though Knox probably lived here only for the few months prior to his death. The museum inside houses many exhibits associated with the life of the great Reformer, and preserves many original features of the building, including a fireplace and a 16thC wall-painting. Open 1000-1700 Mon.-Sat. Apr.-Oct.; 1000-1600 Mon.-Sat. Nov.-Mar. Closed Sun. Last admission 1630/1530. Cost £1.00, 70p child. Bus 1,6,3,21,31,33,34, 35,80,81,82.

Knox, John: (1505-1572) :Born near Haddington, East Lothian, this 16thC leader of the Scottish Reformation was largely responsible for the establishment of the Protestant faith in Scotland. Originally a Roman Catholic priest, he committed himself to Protestantism in 1545, and was Minister of St Giles from 1559 until his death. Although he is remembered principally for intro-ducing the austere doctrines of Calvinism, thus set-ting the pattern of Scottish religious and social life over the following three centuries, he also bequeathed much valuable historical documenta-tion to future generations.

Lady Stair's House: Lady Stair's Close, Lawnmarket, Royal Mile. This house was built in 1622, and sold in 1719 to Elizabeth, Dowager Countess of Stair, from whom it takes its name. Following restoration in 1897, it was presented to the city in 1907, and today houses a literary museum dedicated to three great Scottish writers: Robert Burns, Sir Walter Scott, and Robert Louis Stevenson. Open: Mon.-Sat. 1000-1800, Sun. 1400-1700 Jun.-Sep.; Mon.-Sat. 1000-1700, closed Sun. Oct.-May. Admission free.

Laundry & Dry Cleaning: Most visitors will be content to use the service provided by their hotel, though it is usually faster and cheaper (about 1 hour, and £2 to £3 for a machine-load) to use one of the many coin-operated launderettes to be found in the city. Centrally located launderettes at 13 South Clerk St, 54 Elm Row, 7/11 East London St. Dry cleaners at 123 Hanover St, 23 Frederick St, 6 North Bridge.

Lauriston Castle: 2 Cramond Road South. A late 16thC tower house, with extensive 19thC additions, set in attractive gardens overlooking the Firth of Forth. The interior is preserved as an Edwardian country mansion, with period and reproduction furniture, and a superb collection of Derbyshire Bluejohn ware. Open Apr.-Oct. 1100-1300, 1400-1700 Sat.-Thu.; Nov-Mar: 1400-1600 Sat., Sun., closed Mon.-Fri. Guided tours £1.00 adult, 50p child. Admission to gardens only is free. Free car-park.

Libraries: National Library of Scotland, George IV Bridge, tel: (031) 226 4531. Copyright library, receives a copy of everything published in

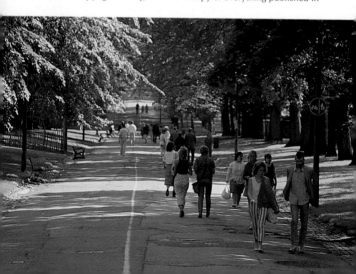

the UK. Reference only. Often holds free exhibitions in entrance hall. Central Library, George IV Bridge, tel: (031) 225 5584. Lending library. Fiction, non-fiction, Scottish Dept, Edinburgh collection, Fine Arts Dept, useful Reference Dept.

Lost Property: Police Lost Property Office, Fettes Avenue, tel: (031) 331 3141. Open 0900-1700 Mon.-Fri. (1800-2000 Mon. only).
British Rail Lost Property Office, Waverley Station, tel: (031) 556 2477. Open 0830-1300, 1400-1700 Mon.-Thu., 0830-1300, 1400-1630 Fri., 0830-1200 Sat. Closed Sun.
Lothian Region Transport, 14 Queen St, tel: (031) 554 4494 and ask for Lost Property Office. Open 0900-1700 Mon.-Fri.
Eastern Scottish Omnibuses, St Andrews Square Bus Station, tel: (031) 556 8126. Open 0830-1230, 1330-1730 Mon.-Fri.

Meadows: A pleasant area of parkland to the south of the city centre, on the site of a drained loch. The International Exhibition of Industry Science and Art was held here in 1886 - remnants include the entrance pillars at the west end of Melville Drive, and the whalebone arch at the end of Jawbone Walk. Today there are trees, paths, a cricket pitch, tennis courts and a children's playground.

Military Tattoo: This spectacular show is held annually on the Castle Esplanade, during the three weeks of the International Festival in August. It is an exciting display of mock battles, fireworks, gymnastics, horsemanship, pageantry and massed pipe bands, and ends movingly with a lone, spotlit piper playing a farewell lament. Information: The Tattoo Office, 1 Cockburn St, tel: (031) 225 1188. Postal bookings accepted from January onward. Counter sales from Ticket Centre, 5 Waverley Bridge, begin in early July. Cost of tickets is £5 to £8.

Money Matters: Banks are generally open 0930-1230, 1330-1530 Mon.-Fri., also 1630-1730 Thu., closed Sat., Sun. Many city centre banks remain open at lunchtime. The Clydesdale Bank at the Tourist Centre, Waverley Market, is open 0830-2030 Mon.-Sat., 1100-1500 Sun., and offers currency exchange facilities, as do a number of city centre banks. A number of English and overseas banks have a branch in the city: Barclays, 35 St Andrews Square; Citibank, 2 Festival Square; Bank of America, 24 St Andrews Square; First National Bank of Chicago, 46 Charlotte Square. There are Currency Exchange Bureaus at Waverley Station, and 23 Princes St. Travellers Cheques are widely accepted throughout Edinburgh and Scotland. you will need your passport when cashing them. It is best to exchange cheques and currency in a bank, as they offer better rates than hotels and exchange bureaus. Credit cards are widely accepted by hotels, restaurants, shops and car-hire companies -- look for their signs in the window. The American Express Office is at 139 Princes St, tel: (031) 225 7881. Open 0900-1700 Mon.-Fri., 0900-1200 Sat.

Most goods and services in the UK are liable to 15% sales tax (called Value Added Tax, or VAT). Foreign visitors may be able to reclaim this tax on any goods they buy, but the procedure is so cumbersome that it is only worthwhile for large purchases. The scheme is run only by certain large stores and speciality shops, whose staff will explain to you what you must do.

Mound, The: This is the name given to the steep hill that winds down to Princes Street from the Royal Mile between Lawnmarket and High Street. It was created during the building of the New Town by the dumping of rubble excavated from the foundations, with the intention of making a short-cut from Old Town to New across the boggy depression of the Nor' Loch (now fully drained and occupied by Princes St Gardens and the railway).

Music: Many kinds of music can be enjoyed in Edinburgh, from classical concerts in the Usher Hall to jazz bands playing in smoky pubs. The music most often associated with Scotland is the 'skirl o' the pipes', and the stirring strains of the massed pipe bands can be enjoyed at the Military Tattoo, and also at the Festival opening parade along Princes St. But don't miss out on Scottish folk music, which ranges from moving historical ballads to toe-tapping fiddle tunes. To find out where to listen to music, ask at the Tourist Centre, or check the listings in *What's On*, *The List*, and the local newspapers. See **What's On.**

New Town: Edinburgh's New Town is a masterpiece of late 18th and early 19thC urban planning, and today forms the largest urban conservation area in Britain. It was begun in the 1780s, after a proposal by George Drummond, Lord Provost of Edinburgh from 1725 to 1764, to ease the overcrowding in the squalid and crime-ridden Old Town as the capital's population steadily increased. The street plan of the original New Town (the regular grid bounded by Queen St, Princes St, St Andrew Square and Charlotte Square) was designed by James Craig, an unknown, self-taught architect only 23 years old. The graceful Georgian terraces, with their regular three-by-four windows, channeled ashlar ground-floor walls, elaborate fanlights, and black-painted wrought-iron lamp-posts and railings attracted the city's upper classes, and such was the New Town's popularity that soon further developments were added, extending north and west as far as Stockbridge, and around the flanks of Calton Hill. Today the New Town is the financial and administrative heart of Edinburgh, with many buildings sensitively converted to offices and banks. But a larger number of buildings remain as desirable private houses and apartments, and the New Town is also a community enjoying the best in elegant, city-centre living.

Newspapers: As well as the full range of national British newspapers, you will find that Scotland has two quality national dailies of its own: the *Glasgow Herald* and *The Scotsman*. The latter is published in Edinburgh, Mon.-Sat., costing 30p, as is the *Evening News* (22p), a local Edinburgh paper containing much useful information. Foreign newspapers and magazines are available from several city-centre newsagents. Try John Menzies on Princes St, or Charles Burns, 367 High St, Royal Mile (opposite St Giles).

Nightlife: Edinburgh's nightlife does not grind to a halt when the Festival ends. All year round there is a wide selection of nightclubs, discos, casinos and bars to entertain those night-owls who enjoy revelling into the small hours. See **ENTERTAINMENT.**

Old Town: The ancient heart of the city, built along the ridge stretching from the Castle Rock to the Palace of Holyroodhouse. The Old Town probably began around the 7th or 8thC as a huddle of cottages close to the castle gates, which gradually spread down the ridge as Edinburgh gained importance as a strategic site. By 1376 the population had grown to 2000. A city wall was built (it crossed the Royal Mile at the foot of the High Street) after the Scottish defeat at Flodden in 1513, and pressure of space meant that houses were built upwards, resulting in the characteristic tall tenement buildings separated by narrow streets and closes. By the 18thC the population was 50,000, and there was much squalor and overcrowding, which led to the decision to build the New Town to the north. Today, renovation has made the Old Town a pleasant place to live, and its atmospheric streets and alleyways are crammed with historic houses, museums, pubs, tearooms and many other attractions.

One O'Clock Gun: Every day, on the dot of 1pm., this Edinburgh institution never fails to make the Princes Street shoppers jump. The tradition of firing a cannon from the Castle battlements at one o'clock began in 1848 to serve as a time signal for ships in the Firth of Forth. In addition, since 1861, the gun has been linked electrically to a time-ball on top of the Nelson Monument on Calton Hill - the ball drops on the stroke of one, thus giving a visual time-signal.

Opening Times: Banks: generally 0930-1230, 1330-1530 Mon.-Fri., and 1630-1800 Thu., closed Sat.-Sun. Some city centre and airport banks open longer hours and at weekends. See **Money Matters.**
Museums and galleries: variable. Check entries in TOPIC and AZ, or consult Tourist Centre.
Office hours: 0900-1700 Mon.-Fri.
Post Offices: 0900-1730 Mon.-Fri., 0900-1230 Sat. closed Sun. Smaller offices may close for lunch 1230-1330.
Pubs: usually 1100-2300 Mon.-Sat., often with late opening until 2400 or 0100 Thu.-Sat. Some pubs close in afternoons 1430-1700. On Sun., most pubs open 1200-1400, 1930-2300. A few will be open all day.
Shops: generally 0900-1730 Mon-Sat, closed Sun. Some small grocery shops open until 2100 and all day Sunday.

Orientation: The city is clustered around the spine of the Royal Mile, which runs eastward from the Castle to Holyroodhouse, below the prominent hill of Arthur's Seat. To the north of the Castle is Princes St and the regular grid-pattern of the New Town. To the south of the Castle, and extending along the Royal Mile is the Old Town. Note that Edinburgh streets often change name several times along their length. For example, the Royal Mile begins as Castlehill, then becomes Lawnmarket, High St, Canongate and Abbey Strand before it reaches Holyrood. And the street that begins as North Bridge at the east end of Princes Street changes its name no less than eight times before it ends at Cameron Toll!

Parking: see Driving.

Parliament House & Law Courts: Parliament Square, High St, Royal Mile. A complex of buildings hidden behind an early 19thC neo-classical facade. One of these, Parliament Hall, was completed in 1639 at the order of Charles I, and was the assembly place of the Scottish Parliament from that time until the Treaty of Union in 1707. It boasts a magnificent, 17thC hammer-beam roof, and stained-glass windows depicting the inauguration of the Court of Session by James V in 1532. Today the Hall and surrounding buildings are the home of the Scottish Law Courts. Open 0930-1630 Tue.-Fri. Admission free.

Passports & Customs Regulations: On arrival in the UK you will need a valid passport. No visas are necessary for EC citizens, Commonwealth citizens (including Australia, Canada and New Zealand), and citizens of the USA and the Republic of South Africa. At Customs, if you have goods to declare over and above your duty-free allowances, you should follow the 'Red Channel' (you must also declare anything you intend to leave or sell in the UK); if you have nothing to declare, follow the 'Green Channel' (which is subject to spot checks by Customs Officers).

Pentland Hills: This range of hills rises to 490 m/1600 ft immediately to the south of Edinburgh, offering pleasant walks and picnics within easy reach of the city. They are also the home of hillend Ski Centre, Britain's longest artificial ski-slope (see **SPORT**).

Petrol: see **Driving**.

Pets: Leave them at home. There are stringent quarantine requirements for imported animals: 6 months, or the entire duration of your stay, if shorter. Any illegally imported animal is liable to be destroyed.

Pharmacies: These are known in Britain as 'Chemists', and are open during normal shop hours. A rota system operates for late opening, and each shop displays a list showing those chemists that will be open late that evening. The main city-centre shop is Boots', 48 Shandwick Place, tel: (031) 225 6757. Police stations will assist in filling an urgent prescription. In a medical emergency, dial 999 and ask for an ambulance.

Photography: Edinburgh is probably Britain's most photogenic city, so don't skimp on film! Most major brands of film are sold in chemists, newsagents, department stores amd souvenir shops. Note that there are usually restrictions on photography in museums and art galleries, so check at the reception desk before snapping away.

Police: British police wear a dark uniform, and black peaked cap with a chequered band. They are not armed, and you will generally find them friendly and helpful in their dealings with visitors. In an emergency, dial 999 and ask for the police. Police HQ in Edinburgh is at Fettes Avenue, tel: (031) 331 3131.

Post Offices: These are indicated by a red sign with yellow lettering. Letter boxes are painted bright red, and display times of collections. Post offices sell stamps for letters and parcels, and there is often a vending machine outside which will sell stamps when the office is closed. Within the UK, letters can be sent either first or second class: first class is slightly more expensive, but should guarantee next-day delivery; second class mail may take several days to arrive. Costs: letters up to 20g, UK and EC: 20p; rest of Europe: 24p; Airmail letters up to 10g, USA: 34p; Australia: 37p.
You can receive mail addressed c/o Poste Restante at the Head Post Office (see below). You will need your passport or other identification when you go to collect it. Head Post Office, 2-4 Waterloo Place, Edinburgh EH1 1AA. Open 0830-1800 Mon.-Fri., 0830-1230 Sat.

Princes Street: One of the most famous and beautiful streets in the world. It dates from the construction of the New Town in the late 18thC, and is unusual in being built-up on one side only, allowing magnificent views to the Castle and Old Town. It began life as an upmarket residential street, but today it is the city main shopping thoroughfare.

Princes Street Gardens: The gardens were laid out in the early 19thC for the residents of Princes St in the newly-built New Town. They occupy the drained site of the former Nor' Loch (North Loch) which once lay beneath the Castle Rock, and have been open to the public since 1850. Points of interest include the Ross Bandstand, where open-air concerts are held in summer; the Floral Clock beside the steps at the foot of The Mound; the Scott Monument; the Scottish-American War

Memorial; and statues of explorer and missionary David Livingstone, and poet Allan Ramsay.

Public Holidays: Fixed holidays: 1 Jan. (New Year's Day); 2 Jan. (Bank Holiday); 25 Dec. (Christmas Day); 26 Dec. (Bank Holiday). Movable holidays: Good Friday (March or April); Spring Bank Holidays (May); August Bank Holiday.
Bank holidays are usually only observed by banks, and most shops and offices remain open.

Public Toilets: In the city centre there are public toilets at: Canongate, Royal Mile; Castle Terrace car-park; Haymarket; corner of Mound and Princes St; St James's Centre; Waverley Market; Ross Bandstand, Princes St Gardens. The 'Superloo' in Waverley Station has showers and shaving points in addition to normal toilet facilities.

Railways: All local and inter-city rail services depart from Waverley Station in the city centre. First class and standard class tickets are available, and special reductions are offered on certain routes. There are frequent and fast services from Edinburgh to London Kings Cross (5hrs, from about £60 return), and Edinburgh to Glasgow (1hr, £7.80 return). There are also regular services to Perth, Dundee, Aberdeen and Inverness. Special tourist tickets offering cut-price travel on trains, buses and ferries in the Scottish Highlands and Islands are also available. For information and timetable enquiries, tel: (031) 556 2451. There is also a helpful Information Desk in Waverley Station.

Religious Services: To find out details of time and place of worship for a variety of religious denominations, contact the Tourist Centre at Waverley Market, tel: 557 1700.

Rose Street: Pedestrian precinct running parallel to Princes St. At one time it was famous for its pubs, and was known as the beer-drinker's golden mile, but today many of the bars have lost their character, and the street is no longer a classic 'pub-crawl'. The Abbotsford (see **PUBS**) and the Kenilworth are still worth a visit, though.

Royal Botanic Garden: Inverleith Row. The history of Edinburgh's Botanic Garden dates back to 1670, making it the second oldest in Britain after Oxford's. From its beginnings as a physic garden established by Edinburgh University's first Professor of Medicine on a small plot of land near to Holyrood Abbey, it was moved several times before arriving at its present 28 ha/70 acre site in 1823. It now receives over 500,000 visitors each year, and is only a 10-minute bus ride from the city centre. It includes an exhibition hall, demonstration gardens, arboretum, peat garden, woodland garden, rock and heath garden, azalea lawn, alpine house, and the largest collection of rhododendrons in the UK. Open Mar-Oct: 0900-1hr before sunset Mon.-Sat., 1100-1hr before sunset Sun.; Oct-Mar: same opening times, but closes at dusk. Admission free. Buses 8, 19, 23, 27, 39.

Royal Mile: The narrow, 1,984-yard long cobbled street that runs downhill from the Castle entrance to the gates of Holyroodhouse, and forms the backbone of Edinburgh's Old Town. So named because it was the route followed by the royal carriages that conveyed kings and queens between the Palace and the Castle.

St Giles Cathedral: High St, Royal Mile. Strictly speaking, this church should be referred to as the High Kirk of Edinburgh. It was a cathedral proper only during the years 1633-38 and 1661-89, but the name has stuck. There has been a church on this site since 854, but most of the present-day structure dates from 1829-33, when the exterior was faced in smooth stone. The four central pillars within date from the 12thC, the choir from 1460, and the impressive crown spire from 1495. The ornate Gothic Thistle Chapel was added in 1909-11. The famous Reformer, John Knox, was Minister here from 1559 until his death in 1572. Open 0900-1900 (1700 in winter) Mon.-Sat., later on Sun. Public worship: 1200 Mon.-Sat.; 0800, 1000, 1130, 1800, 2000 Sun. Admission to kirk is free; to Thistle Chapel 30p , 5p child. Buses 1, 6, 34, 35.

Salisbury Crags: The impressive line of cliffs that rises above the city to the west of Arthur's Seat. An enjoyable walk, known as the Radical Road, runs along the foot of the cliffs. See **WALK 3.**

Scotch Whisky Heritage Centre: 358 Castlehill, Royal Mile. An exhibition with audio-visual displays and theatrical sets describing the industrial and social history of Scotch whisky, from its 17thC beginnings to the present day. Open Apr-Oct: daily 0900-1900; Nov-Mar: 0900-1700. Closed Christmas Day and New Year Day. Cost £2.50, £1.25 child. Buses 1, 6, 23, 27, 30, 34, 35, 40, 41, 42, 46, 89.

Scott Monument: East Princes St Gardens. An elaborate Gothic spire towering 61m/200ft above Princes St, built in 1840-46 as a memorial to one of Scotland's best-loved novelists, Sir Walter Scott (1771-1832). The ornate exterior includes carvings of characters from Scott's novels, and at the bottom is a 30-ton white marble statue of

Scott with his dog, Maida. You can climb the 287 steps to the top and enjoy magnificent views of the city. Open 0900-1500 Mon-Sat. Cost 45p.

Scott, Sir Walter: One of Scotland's most famous writers, Scott (1771-1832) was born and educated in Edinburgh. He lived at 28 Castle St in the New Town for 28 years, before moving to the country house of Abbotsford in the Borders. His works include the romantic poem *The Lady of the Lake*, and the novels *Ivanhoe* and *Rob Roy*. He is buried in Dryburgh Abbey, near Abbotsford. See **EXCURSION 2**.

Sports: The most popular spectator sport in Scotland is Association Football (soccer). Edinburgh has two major teams, Heart of Midlothian FC and Hibernian FC. There are regular Saturday and Wednesday matches in season (winter) at their respective grounds: Tynecastle (off Gorgie Rd), and Easter Road (north of London Rd). Rugby Union is played at Murrayfield Stadium (off Corstorphine Rd), which hosts matches in the annual Five Nations international competition. There are occasional national and international athletics meets at Meadowbank Stadium, London Rd, motor-racing at Ingliston Race-track (west of the city), and horse-racing at Musselburgh (east of the city). See also **SPORTS**.

Stevenson, Robert Louis: This world-famous writer (1850-94) was born at 8 Howard Place, opposite the Royal Botanic Garden, and lived for about 30 years at 17 Heriot Row in the New Town. He qualified as an advocate at Edinburgh University in 1867, but made his name as a writer with such works as *A Child's Garden of Verse*, *Treasure Island*, *Kidnapped* and *The Strange Case of Dr Jekyll and Mr Hyde*. He also wrote the words of the well-known *Skye Boat Song*. He died in Samoa, in the South Pacific, and is buried there.

Students: Bring your International Student Identity Card - it will allow you to claim discounts on certain kinds of bus and rail travel, and on admission to certain museums, exhibitions *etc*. Your university union may have reciprocal rights with those of Edinburgh and Heriot-

Watt Universities, in which case you will be able to use their facilities, including inexpensive cafeterias, bars, showers, TV lounges *etc*. Edinburgh University Unions are at Teviot Row, Bristo Square; Chambers St; and Kings Buildings, West Mains Rd. Heriot Watt University Union is at 23 Grindlay St.

Talbot Rice Art Gallery: Old College, South Bridge. Houses Edinburgh University's permanent art collection, including some notable 17th-centruy Dutch paintings, and 16th and 17thC bronzes. Open 1000-1700 Mon.-Sat. Closed Sun. Admission free. Buses 3, 7, 8, 21, 31, 33, 80, 81, 82, 87, 89.

Taxis: Like London, Edinburgh's taxis are distinctive black 'Hackney carriages'. The yellow 'For Hire' sign on the roof is lit when the cab is available. They can be hailed in the street, ordered by telephone, or found at one of the many taxi-ranks throughout the city-centre. The main ranks are at Waverley Station (where there are often long queues), Haymarket Station, West End, St Andrew Square Bus Station, and most of the side streets off Princes Street. It can be very difficult to find a taxi during Friday and Saturday evenings. Basic charge of 90p, plus 10p for every 315 m/345 yds (equivalent to around 50p/mile or 30p/km). Telephone numbers of 24-hour radio taxis: Castle Cabs (031) 228 2555; Central Radio Taxis (031) 229 5221; City Cabs (031) 228 1211.

Telephones & Telegrams: Public pay-phones are common throughout the city. The older blue pay-phones accept 2p, 10p and 50p coins, while the more modern, single-slot machines, which are replacing the older ones, accept all coins except 1p. Instructions for use are clearly displayed in the phone booth. You can make local, long-distance and international calls from all telephones, either dialling direct or through the operator (UK operator, dial 100; international operator 155). Telephones with a green 'Phonecard' sign can only be used with a plastic card available from post offices and newsagents in £1, £5 and £10 versions. In the UK, a 'collect' call is known as a reverse-charge call.
To make an international call, dial 010 followed by the country code

(USA & Canada 1, Australia 61, New Zealand 64, France 33, West Germany 49), then the area code, minus the initial zero, and the number. Full instructions can be found in any telephone directory. A wide selection of overseas directories can be consulted in the reference department of the Central Library (see **Libraries**).

The cheapest time to make UK calls is 1800-0600 weekdays, and during the weekend. Local call costs around 10p for 3 minutes. Cost of 3-minute call to London is 30p; USA 200p; France & Germany 110p; Australia 300p.

Telegrams: all telegrams must be dictated by telephone; there is no longer a traditional counter service. Dial 100 and ask for Telemessage (for UK and USA) or International Telegrams (rest of world).

Time Differences: The British Isles use Greenwich Mean Time from late October to late March, and British Summer Time (GMT plus 1 hour) from March to October. At noon in Edinburgh, in summer, it is: 0700 in New York and Montreal; 0400 in Los Angeles and Vancouver; 2100 in Sydney; 2300 in Auckland; 1300 in Paris and Bonn.

Tipping: Hotels and restaurants often include a service charge in your bill. Where service is not included, it is custimary to leave a tip of 10-15% to waiting staff. A porter gets 30-50p per bag. Taxi drivers often get 10-15% of the fare, and hairdressers 10% of the bill. Tipping is not expected in theatres, cinemas and petrol stations.

Tourist Information: The main source of information and advice for visitors to the city is the Tourist Information and Accommodation Centre at Waverley Market, Princes St, tel: (031) 557 2727. It includes an accommodation reservation service, and a bank with currency exchange facilities. Open 0830-2000 Mon.-Sat., 1100-2000 Sun. (open daily until 2100 July-Aug.). There is another office at Edinburgh Airport. Scottish Travel Centre, South St Andrew St. tel: (031) 332 2433. Open same hours as Tourist Centre. Provides information and advice on travel and tourism in the rest of Scotland, including tours and excursions. Scottish Tourist Board, 23 Ravelston Terrace, Edinburgh EH4 3EU, tel: (031) 343 2433. Postal and telephone enquiries only. Provides informa-

tion on all aspects of tourism in Scotland. The STB has a London office at 19 Cockspur Road, London SW1Y 5BL, tel: (01) 930 8661.

Transport: Edinburgh is a fairly small city with a compact central area where most of the major attractions are concentrated. It is probably best explored on foot. For longer trips within the city, use the efficient bus system (see **Bus & Coach Services**). For destinations outside Edinburgh, the choice is between bus and train. The latter is usually faster and more comfortable, but also more expensive. See **Railways**.

Traveller's Cheques: see Money Matters

University of Edinburgh: Founded under the Royal Charter of James VI in 1583, Edinburgh's University is the sixth-oldest in Britain. It is also Scotland's biggest private owner of buildings. Its original site on the corner of Chambers St and South Bridge is known as Old College, and now houses the Law Faculty. Other main sites are at George Sq. (Arts and Social Science), New College, on The Mound (Divinity), Teviot Place (Medicine) and Kings Buildings, West Mains Road (Science). The University has 11,000 students, and enjoys a world reputation for excellence in medicine and science. Famous graduates from the past include Charles Darwin, Arthur Conan Doyle, Sir Walter Scott, and Robert Louis Stevenson.

Water of Leith: This is the small river whose deep, wooded valley cuts through the heart of the city. See **WALK 4**.

Waverley Market: A modern, enclosed shopping arcade next to Waverley Station. The principal Tourist Information Centre is situated at street level.

Waverley Station: Edinburgh's main-line railway station, situated towards the east end of Princes St. For information and timetable enquiries, tel: (031) 556 2451. Station facilities include restaurant, bar, newsagent, accommodation desk, exchange bureau, left luggage, car-hire desk, and toilets with showers and shaver-points.

What's On: To find out what's happening on the city's entertainment scene, consult the following publications: *What's On In Edinburgh*, a free monthly booklet, available from Tourist Centre, listing current events, exhibitions, entertainment.; *The List*, fortnightly, cost 60p from newsagents, contains detailed list of events and entertainments in Glasgow and Edinburgh - cinema, theatre, music, art, rock, sport. *Evening News*, daily Mon.-Sat., cost 22p from newsagents and street vendors, is a local newspaper with useful restaurants and entertainment section.

Youth Hostels: The Scottish Youth Hostels Association has two hostels in Edinburgh, which are open to visitors with a national or international membership card: Bruntsfield YH, 7 Bruntsfield Crescent, tel: (031) 447 2994. Eglinton YH, 18 Eglinton Crescent, tel: (031) 337 1120.
There is an Independent Hostel at 8 Blackfriars St, tel: (031) 557 3984. No membership needed. Open 0630-0230. Cost £4.50/night, self-catering, free use of kitchen. Hot showers.
YMCA, Princes St, tel: (031) 225 1174. YWCA, Randolph Crescent, tel: (031) 225 4379.